Fluency Quick Checks

Table of Contents

Assessing Fluency

Quick Check Assessments

Introduction

Reading fluency is the ability to read texts quickly, accurately, and with appropriate expression. A proficient reader can read a text fluently and with comprehension.

This book is intended to help teachers assess students' oral reading fluency on a regular basis.

The ongoing assessment of oral reading fluency allows the teacher to establish a benchmark for each student and monitor progress over time. Ongoing fluency assessments (informal fluency-related tasks, teacher observations, and formal assessments) also enable educators to determine whether instructional goals have been met.

Benchmark's *Fluency Quick Checks* provide a set of carefully calibrated reading passages for Kindergarten through Grade 6. There are fifteen reading passages for Grades K–1 and ten passages per grade for Grades 2–6. Each reading passage has been developed to fit a specific reading level and passage length appropriate for students at various levels of proficiency. Reading levels in Kindergarten and early first grade are based primarily on the timely introduction of level-appropriate phonic elements, the use of high-frequency words taught in the Benchmark program, and Lexile measures. In Grades 1–6, reading levels are based primarily on Lexile measures. The table below describes general ranges for Lexiles and passage length at each grade.

Lexile Ranges and Passage Length

Grade	Lexile Range	Passage Length
K	100L–160L	50–90 words
1	150L–380L	60–130 words
2	360L–530L	90–150 words
3	530L–810L	120–160 words
4	670L–850L	130–170 words
5	820L–990L	140–190 words
6	900L–1050L	140–200 words

There is some overlap in reading level between the end of one grade and the beginning of another. Students at any grade level may be assessed with any of these passages. In Grades K–3, the passages are divided evenly between narrative and informative genres. Grades 4–6 have more informative passages than narrative texts. Each passage also has a set of comprehension questions to monitor students' understanding of what they read.

Each assessment has a Student Page and a Teacher Page. The Student Page may be handed to the student for reading aloud. The Teacher Page may be used by the teacher to record the results of the student's oral reading, check the student's comprehension, and determine the student's reading rate. Each assessment passage may be used to evaluate:

• Oral Reading Accuracy (the percentage of words in a passage that are read correctly)

• Reading Rate (the number of words read correctly per minute)

• Comprehension (the number of questions answered correctly)

• Fluency (a combination of phrasing, intonation, and expression)

Teachers may evaluate any or all of these elements with a single assessment. Use the assessments in the most appropriate and most helpful way for your situation. The directions provided in the next section explain how to evaluate each element.

We recommend that teachers formally assess students' reading fluency at least three times: at the beginning, in the middle, and at the end of the school year. We have provided fifteen passages for Grades K–1 and ten passages per grade for Grades 2–6 to facilitate more frequent assessment, if desired, and to provide follow-up assessments for students who might need additional instruction or practice. Assessment information can become part of students' permanent portfolio for documentation and accountability. Students may be assessed individually when most convenient for teachers—at the beginning or end of the day, or when appropriate during a portion of small-group reading time, or when students are engaged in independent reading.

Directions for Administering Oral Reading Fluency Assessments

To administer an assessment, identify the most appropriate starting level for the student. All of the passages in this book are arranged sequentially by level of difficulty in each grade. You can begin with an assessment at the student's independent reading level (95–98% accuracy) to establish a benchmark at the beginning of the year. If you are not sure of the student's reading level, you may want to begin with a passage that is below grade level. Subsequent assessments can be used to monitor progress during the school year.

Once you have determined the assessment level, make a copy of the Student Page and Teacher Page at that level. You may create a folder for each student to help organize and document oral reading assessments. Throughout the year, store the students' assessments in these folders, or place the assessments in individual student portfolios. You may also want to record results for all students in the classroom on the Oral Reading Rate Progress Record (page xiv).

The following directions explain how to use the passages in this book to assess oral reading accuracy, reading rate, comprehension, and fluency.

How to Assess Oral Reading Accuracy and Rate

Reading accuracy and rate may be assessed whenever a student reads aloud. Use the procedure below.

1. Make a copy of the Student Page with a fluency assessment passage at the student's independent reading level (95–98% accuracy). You will also need a copy of the Teacher Page to use for recording the results of the assessment.

2. Give the reading passage to the student. Ask the student to read the passage using his or her best voice. Make note of the starting time.

3. As the student reads, mark any errors with a slash mark through the words. Use the scoring guidelines below.

4. At the end of one minute, mark the point in the text where the student was reading by circling the last word read. Allow the student to finish reading the passage. Or, have the student read the entire passage and mark the total amount of time required.

5. To determine reading rate: Count the number of words read correctly in one minute. This is the student's reading rate. Record this information on the Teacher Page as words per minute. Or, using the total reading time, apply this formula to calculate the reading rate:

   Total # of words read ÷ # of seconds × 60 = _____ words per minute

6. To determine reading accuracy: Count the total number of words read correctly and divide this number by the total number of words in the passage. Then multiply by 100. This is the percentage of words read accurately. You can use the formula below.

   For example, if a student makes 6 errors in a passage that has 90 words, then you would calculate as follows:

   90 − 6 = 84 ÷ 90 = 0.93 × 100 = 93%

   Record this number in the scoring box on the Teacher Page.

7. Use the following table to compare the student's performance to the reading rate goal for the grade level and time of year. Document this on the Teacher Page.

Reading Rate Goals
(words per minute)

Grade	Beginning of Year	Middle of Year	End of Year
1	20	35	60
2	65	80	95
3	95	105	115
4	115	115	120
5	120	125	130
6	135	140	145

Adapted from Hasbrouck & Tindal (2006)

How to Assess Reading Accuracy

Words read correctly include words that are self-corrected within three seconds of an error. (Mark each self-correction with SC above the word.) Correctly read words that are repeated are not counted as errors. Errors include:

- Mispronounced words—words that are misread.

- Word substitutions—one word read for another word. For example, *boat* for *ship*.

- Omissions or skipped words—words that are not read.

- Hesitations—If the student hesitates for three seconds or longer, say the word and have the student continue reading.

How to Assess Comprehension

A student who reads a passage fluently should be able to demonstrate general comprehension of the passage. The student should not be expected to remember every factual detail after one reading, but he or she should understand what the passage is about, the main points made in the passage, and the connections between events or ideas. The comprehension questions for each passage have been developed with these guidelines in mind.

To assess the student's comprehension, ask each of the comprehension questions on the Teacher Page. As the student responds, compare the response to the sample correct response given with the question. Mark each question correct or incorrect. If a question has multiple answers, you may want to give students half-credit for giving at least one correct response.

Each passage has three comprehension questions. Students should answer at least two of the three questions correctly to demonstrate adequate comprehension.

You may want to make note of the student's incorrect responses during the assessment. Reviewing these responses afterward can help you determine what the student does or does not understand, and may possibly give you helpful information regarding the additional instruction the student may need. For example, if a question asks what the passage is mostly about and a student answers with a factual detail rather than the main topic, then follow-up instruction may focus on the difference between the main topic and detail sentences.

How to Assess Oral Fluency

Oral reading fluency incorporates a number of elements, including phrasing, intonation, and expression. The oral fluency rubric below may be used to help judge a student's overall reading fluency beyond reading rate, accuracy, and comprehension. Information derived from using this rubric may be helpful in deciding how to assist students to improve their reading skills. If you apply this rubric during a student's oral reading, record the result on the Teacher Page by circling the 1, 2, 3, or 4 next to Fluency.

Rating	Characteristics
1	Reads word by word. Does not attend to the author's syntax or sentence structure. Reads with a monotone voice.
	Does not express emotions or intonation indicated by punctuation marks. In reading fiction, does not recognize dialogue or distinguish between characters.
2	Reads slowly and in a choppy manner, usually in two-word phrases. Gives some attention to the author's syntax and sentence structures.
	Reads with some intonation and some attention to punctuation. At times reads in a monotone voice.
	Occasionally expresses emotion, differentiates between dialogue and regular text, or distinguishes between characters.
3	Reads in phrases of three or four words. Uses appropriate syntax.
	Reads by adjusting intonation appropriately. Consistently attends to punctuation.
	Frequently expresses emotion, differentiates between dialogue and regular text, and distinguishes between characters.
4	Reads in longer, more meaningful phrases. Regularly uses pitch, stress, and author's syntax to reflect comprehension.
	Reads with intonation that reflects feeling, anticipation, tension, character development, and mood. Consistently attends to punctuation.

Scoring Key

A student who scores 1 or 2 has not achieved an appropriate level of fluency for the level of the passage. A student who scores a 3 is very close to reading fluency at the level of the passage. A student who scores a 4 has achieved reading fluency for the level at which the passage is written.

Interpreting Results

Passages in this assessment book may be used to evaluate oral reading accuracy, reading rate, comprehension, and fluency and phrasing. All four of these elements are integral to oral reading fluency, and all of them may be helpful in evaluating a student's reading fluency and planning for instruction. In general, a student who reads at the independent reading level and meets the reading rate goal will also score well in comprehension and will read with appropriate fluency and phrasing. For a student whose scores are not definitive indicators of reading fluency level, or a student who scores well in two of these areas but not in the other two, we recommend follow-up assessment and classroom observation to clarify instructional needs.

Based on your student's score, you may decide to offer the student additional resources as in the *Benchmark Advance Intervention.* The Resource Map that follows this introduction aligns the skills being assessed to the *Intervention* lessons.

If the student scores...	Then...
100% (4/4)	Move on to the next Quick Check or skill.
75% (3/4)	Consider administering the Quick Check again. Continue monitoring the student during future Quick Checks.
50% or lower (2/4 or less)	Use additional resources shown in the Resource Map to provide the student with opportunities to remediate skills.

Fluency Quick Check Resource Map

Fluency Skills	Quick Check	*Benchmark Advance Intervention Fluency* Lessons
Grades K–1		
Read with Understanding, Intonation, and Expression	1–15	**Grade K** Lesson 1–15A. Read with Understanding, Intonation, and Expression
Read with Accuracy, Intonation, and Expression	1–15	**Grade K** Lesson 1–15B. Read with Accuracy, Appropriate Rate, and Expression
Read to Confirm Word Recognition and Understanding	1–15	**Grade K** Lesson 1–13C. Read to Confirm Word Recognition and Understanding
Read Informational Text with Understanding, Intonation, and Expression	9, 15	**Grade 1** Lessons 1A. Read Informational Text with Understanding, Intonation, and Expression
Read Literary Text with Understanding, Intonation, and Expression	1–8, 10–14	**Grade 1** Lessons 2A. Read Literary Text with Understanding, Intonation, and Expression
Grade 2		
Read Informational Text with Understanding, Intonation, and Expression	16, 18, 22–23	Lessons 1A. Read Informational Text with Understanding, Intonation, and Expression
Read Literary Text with Understanding, Intonation, and Expression	17, 19–21	Lessons 2A. Read Literary Text with Understanding, Intonation, and Expression
Grade 3		
Read Informational Text with Understanding, Intonation, and Expression	28, 30, 32–33, 35	Lessons 1A. Read Informational Text with Understanding, Intonation, and Expression
Read Literary Text with Understanding, Intonation, and Expression	26–27, 29, 31, 34	Lessons 2A. Read Literary Text with Understanding, Intonation, and Expression

Fluency Skills	Quick Check	*Benchmark Advance Intervention Fluency* Lessons
Grade 4		
Read Informational Text with Understanding, Intonation, and Expression	36, 38–39, 43–45	**Grades 4–6** Lessons 1A. Read Informational Text with Understanding, Intonation, and Expression
Read Literary Text with Understanding, Intonation, and Expression	37, 40–42	**Grades 4–6** Lessons 2A. Read Literary Text with Understanding, Intonation, and Expression
Grade 5		
Read Informational Text with Understanding, Intonation, and Expression	47, 49–50, 51, 53–55	**Grades 4–6** Lessons 1A. Read Informational Text with Understanding, Intonation, and Expression
Read Literary Text with Understanding, Intonation, and Expression	46, 48, 52	**Grades 4–6** Lessons 2A. Read Literary Text with Understanding, Intonation, and Expression
Grade 6		
Read Informational Text with Understanding, Intonation, and Expression	56, 58–59, 61, 63–65	**Grades 4–6** Lessons 1A. Read Informational Text with Understanding, Intonation, and Expression
Read Literary Text with Understanding, Intonation, and Expression	57, 60, 62	**Grades 4–6** Lessons 2A. Read Literary Text with Understanding, Intonation, and Expression

Additional Teacher Resources

The following resources have been added to help you track student progress over time, provide additional guidance for evaluating fluency, allow students the opportunity for critical self-evaluation, and suggest alternative fluency assessments. These documents are not essential for administering the Quick Checks and are included as a way to support and extend your fluency instruction and intervention.

Fluency Development over Time

Developmental Reading Stages	Observable Reading Behaviors
Emergent	Fluently reads some high-frequency words (15–20) Decoding consonants and short vowels Beginning to attend to ending punctuation Beginning to read with expression and intonation
Early	Fluently reads many high-frequency words (100–150) Decoding blends, digraphs, diphthongs Uses ending punctuation, quotation marks Developing expression and intonation when reading
Transitional	Fluently reads a large number of high-frequency words (150–350+) Beginning to decode multisyllabic words Attends to punctuation for phrasing Uses understanding of grammatical structures to adjust fluency when reading Integrates word recognition, decoding, and expression more consistently when reading
Advanced	Utilizes an expanding bank of high-frequency words (350+) Decodes multisyllabic words consistently Uses word-solving strategies to maintain comprehension and fluent reading of text Uses text structure and genre features to adjust fluency when reading Consistently integrates accuracy, rate, and prosody when reading

Oral Reading Rate Progress Record

Teacher Name: _____ Grade Level: _____

Student Name	Beginning of Year (WPM)	Midyear (WPM)	End of Year (WPM)

Grades K–6 • Benchmark Advance • **Fluency** Quick Checks • © Benchmark Education Company, LLC

Using Integrated Fluency

Fluency Rubrics are used to identify how students are integrating all aspects of fluency (accuracy, rate, prosody) as they read aloud. Other assessment tools such as the NAEP Oral Reading Fluency Scale (Pinnell et al., 1995) and the fluency scoring guide (Rasinski & Zutell, 1991) are additional tools to reference when assessing oral reading fluency. Use the following Fluency Rubric to note accuracy, rate, prosody, and how students are integrating them together for comprehension and fluent reading. As you conduct informal reading conferences or anytime you listen to students read aloud from an independent or instructional level text, you can use the rubric for consistently evaluating their fluency progress.

Fluency Rubric

Student: _____ Date: _____

The key elements of reading fluency—accuracy, speed, pacing, pausing, inflection/intonation, expression, phrasing, and the integration of these skills—may be assessed anytime a student reads aloud. Discuss the assessment rubric, modeling each description, so students know what you expect.

Rating Scale	Elements of Fluent Reading
	Accuracy
1	Multiple attempts at decoding words without success. Word reading accuracy is inadequate/poor (below 90%).
2	Attempts to self-correct errors, usually unsuccessful. Word reading accuracy is marginal (90%–93%).
3	Attempts to self-correct errors are successful. Word reading accuracy is good (94%–97%).
4	Most words are read correctly on initial attempt. Minimal self-corrections all successful. Word reading accuracy is excellent (98%–100%).
	Rate: Speed, Pacing, Pausing
1	Slow and laborious reading.
2	Reading is either moderately slow or inappropriately fast; pausing is infrequent or ignored.
3	Unbalanced combination of slow and fast reading containing inconsistent pausing.
4	Reading is consistently natural, conversational, and appropriately varied (resembling natural oral language).
	Prosody: Inflection/Intonation and Expression
1	Reads in an inexpressive, monotone manner and does not attend to punctuation.
2	Reads with some intonation (pitch/tone/volume/stress) and some attention to punctuation. Reads in a monotone at times.
3	Reads by adjusting intonation (pitch/tone/volume/stress) with minor errors. Consistently attends to punctuation.
4	Reads with intonation that reflects feeling, anticipation, tension, character development, and mood.
	Prosody: Phrasing
1	Reads word by word. Does not attend to author's syntax or sentence structures. Has limited sense of phrase boundaries.
2	Reads slowly and in a choppy manner, usually in two-word phrases. Some attention is given to author's syntax and sentence structures.
3	Reads in phrases of three to four words. Appropriate syntax is used.
4	Reads in longer, more meaningful phrases. Regularly uses phrase boundaries, punctuation, sentence structure, and author's syntax to reflect comprehension and fluent reading.
	Integration
1	Reading is monotone, laborious, and inexpressive, and accuracy rate is poor (below 90%).
2	Reading is unbalanced, with inconsistent rate and pacing, some phrasing, inadequate intonation and expression, and marginal accuracy (90%–93%).
3	Reading is somewhat adjusted with some variation in rate, appropriate prosody, and with good accuracy (94%–97%).
4	Reads in an integrated manner with high accuracy, rate, intonation, and expression on a consistent basis. Fluent reading reflects understanding and interpretation of text.

Fluency Self-Assessment Instructions

"Assessing metacognition allows us to discover students' perceptions of themselves as readers and writers, the reading and writing they do, and the strategies they employ to solve the problems they encounter in reading and writing."

—Rhodes & Shanklin, 1993

The Fluency Self-Assessment Checklist can be used with students of all ages to promote reflection and goal setting for improving fluent reading. Younger students can use the form with happy/sad faces and older students the yes/no response version. These same prompts can be used as you conduct individual reading conferences with students as prompts for student reflection and evaluation of their reading performance. After completing the self-assessment, students can use the checklist to identify areas in need of reinforcement and set goals for improving the various aspects of fluency, including speed/pacing, pausing, inflection/intonation, phrasing, expression, and integration of accuracy, rate, and prosody. Discuss with students the connection between how they read a particular text and the impact on comprehension.

Name: _____   Date: _____

Fluency Self-Assessment Checklist

	☺	☹
Speed/Pacing		
Did my speed and pacing match the kind of text I was reading?	❏	❏
Did my speed and pacing match what the author was saying?	❏	❏
Did I read in a natural talking sound?	❏	❏
Did I slow my reading down when appropriate?	❏	❏
Did I pay attention to punctuation?	❏	❏
Pausing		
Did I pause to keep from running all my words together?	❏	❏
Did I pause in the correct locations?	❏	❏
Did I pause for the appropriate length of time?	❏	❏
Did I pause to help my reading make sense?	❏	❏
Did I use punctuation to help me figure out when to pause?	❏	❏
Inflection/Intonation		
Did I make my voice rise at a question mark?	❏	❏
Did I make my voice fall at a period?	❏	❏
Did I think about what the author was saying so I would know when to read louder or softer?	❏	❏
Did I think about what the author was saying so I would know when to stress or emphasize words?	❏	❏
Phrasing		
Did I notice the phrases?	❏	❏
Did I read all the words in each phrase together?	❏	❏
Did I think about what the words in the phrase mean when they are together?	❏	❏
Expression		
Did I look for clues so I could anticipate the mood of the passage?	❏	❏
Did I use my tone of voice, facial expressions, and body language to express what the author or characters were thinking or feeling?	❏	❏
Did I change my reading when something new was about to happen?	❏	❏
Integration		
Did I read the words right? (accuracy)	❏	❏
Did I read the words at the right speed? (rate)	❏	❏
Did I read with expression? (prosody)	❏	❏
Did my reading sound like talking?	❏	❏
Did I understand what I read?	❏	❏

Assessing Reader's Theater Performance

Reader's Theater and oral presentations provide opportunities for students to model fluent reading. Rubrics and checklists can be used before, during, and after performances to improve fluency and to help students prepare for final public performances.

Use the Reader's Theater Assessment Rubric during individual conferences or after a performance to assess students' understanding of characterization. The rubric includes a rating scale for assessing the following:

Phrasing and Fluency

Intonation

Pace

Listening

Reader's Theater Assessment Rubric

Rating Scale	Phrasing and Fluency
1	Reads word by word. Does not attend to the author's syntax or sentence structures.
2	Reads slowly and in a choppy manner, usually in two-word phrases. Some attention is given to the author's syntax and sentence structures.
3	Reads in phrases of three or four words. Appropriate syntax is used.
4	Reads in longer, more meaningful phrases. Regularly uses pitch, stress, and author's syntax to reflect comprehension.
	Intonation
1	Reads with a monotone voice.
2	Reads with some intonation and some attention to punctuation. At times reads in a monotone voice.
3	Reads by adjusting intonation appropriately. Consistently attends to punctuation.
4	Reads with intonation that reflects feeling, anticipation, tension, character development, and mood.
	Listening
1	Does not listen attentively and cannot provide relevant suggestions to improve readings of others. Is disruptive.
2	Listens most of the time but has difficulty commenting on the readings of others.
3	Listens to the readings of others without interruption. Makes some suggestions for ways to improve readings. Needs help clarifying own ideas and ideas of others.
4	Listens to the readings of others without interruption. Comments positively on the readings and makes appropriate suggestions for improvement. Seeks clarification when something is not understood. Clarifies own comments when not understood by others, using such phrasing as "what I meant was..."
	Pace
1	Slow and laborious reading.
2	Reading is either moderately slow or inappropriately fast.
3	Unbalanced combination of slow and fast reading.
4	Reading is consistently natural, conversational, and appropriate (resembling natural oral language).

After a Reader's Theater performance, ask students to use the Self-Assessment form appropriate for their level to monitor and evaluate their reading and performance of a script.

Reader's Theater Self-Assessment (Levels A–E)

Student: _____   Script: _____

Character I Portray: _____   Date: _____

1. Did my reading sound like talking?

   ☺   😐   ☹

2. Did I use my voice to show the character's feelings?

   ☺   😐   ☹

3. Did I say the lines as the character would say them?

   ☺   😐   ☹

4. Did I use the punctuation marks to help me know how to say the words?

   ☺   😐   ☹

5. Did I read with a good speed?

   ☺   😐   ☹

6. Did I fix my mistakes when I read?

   ☺   😐   ☹

7. Did I act like my character?

   ☺   😐   ☹

8. Did I listen carefully to the other readers?

   ☺   😐   ☹

Reader's Theater Self-Assessment (Levels F–M)

Student: _____ Script: _____

Character I Portray: _____ Date: _____

Please read each item and think about how fluently you read the character's lines. Place a mark next to either **yes** or **no** on the lines provided. Talk to your teacher about items you need more help with in rehearsal.

Did I make my reading sound like talking? _____ **yes** _____ **no**

Did I read in phrases? _____ **yes** _____ **no**

Did I use my voice to show the character's feelings? _____ **yes** _____ **no**

Did I say the lines as the character would? _____ **yes** _____ **no**

Did my voice change to show that I read the punctuation marks? _____ **yes** _____ **no**

Did I read with a good speed? _____ **yes** _____ **no**

Did I fix my mistakes when I read? _____ **yes** _____ **no**

Did I act like the character? _____ **yes** _____ **no**

Reader's Theater Self-Assessment (Levels N–X)

Student: _____ Script: _____

Character I Portray: _____ Date: _____

Please read each item and think about how fluently you read the character's lines. As you read through each element of fluency, mark **yes** or **no** responses on the lines provided. At the bottom, tell how you plan to improve your reading in the areas where you answered **no**. Make comments or give examples of how well you read, and list any areas where you could receive more help.

1. As I read, did I read for phrasing and fluency by:
   - reading in longer, meaningful phrases? _____
   - paying attention to the author's language patterns (words, sentences)? _____
   - making the reading sound like dialogue or natural oral language? _____
   - stressing certain words to emphasize/reveal the importance of a word or phrase? _____

2. As I read, did I use intonation by:
   - using my voice to make the reading reflect the feelings, anticipation, tension, mood, and personality of the character? _____
   - paying attention to punctuation? _____
   - interpreting the punctuation and using my voice to appropriately raise or lower its sound because of the type of sentence/punctuation I read? _____

3. As I read, did I pay attention to pace by:
   - using an appropriate speed of reading? _____
   - reading the lines with the same speed and flow that I use when I talk? _____
   - reading with very few hesitations or unnecessary pauses and repetitions? _____

4. As I read, did I read accurately by:
   - quickly recognizing words and reading them correctly? _____
   - really thinking about the meaning of the story and known words (high-frequency words, sight words, etc.) and word parts as anchors to help me figure out unknown words? _____
   - self-correcting any miscues or errors on my first try/attempt? _____
   - making the words sound meaningful? _____

5. As I read, did I really try to understand the character and read and say the lines the same way the character probably would by:
   - making inferences about the character? _____
   - using my voice (tone) to sound like the character? _____
   - using my voice to express a particular feeling of the character? _____
   - using body language (gestures) to better express the feelings of the character? _____
   - using appropriate facial expressions in a way that would best represent the character? _____

Plan of Action: I will work on improving my reading fluency during the repeated readings of my character lines by:

_____

_____

_____

When reading independently, I feel...

_____

I would like my teacher or a peer to help me with...

1. _____

2. _____

3. _____

Reader's Theater Fluency Self-Assessment

Student: _____ Script: _____

Character I Portray: _____ Date: _____

Complete the rubric below. Tell how you plan to improve your reading fluency in the areas where you answered **no**.

Skill	Behavior	Yes	No
Fluency and Phrasing	I read in longer, meaningful phrases.		
	I paid attention to the author's language patterns.		
	I made the reading sound like dialogue.		
	I stressed certain words to emphasize their importance.		
Intonation	I used my voice to make the reading reflect feeling, anticipation, tension, mood, and the personality of my character.		
	I paid attention to punctuation.		
	I raised or lowered my voice to interpret the punctuation of sentences.		
Pacing	I used an appropriate speed of reading.		
	I read the lines with the same speed and flow that I use when I talk.		
	I read with very few hesitations or unnecessary pauses and repetitions.		
Accuracy	I recognized words quickly and read them correctly.		
	I really thought about the meaning of the story and known words and word parts to help me figure out unknown words.		
	I corrected myself when I made an error.		
Character Analysis	I made the words sound meaningful.		
	I made inferences about my character.		
	I used my voice (tone) to sound like the character.		
	I used my voice to express a particular feeling of the character.		
	I used body language (gestures) to better express the feelings of the character.		
	I used appropriate facial expressions to represent my character.		

Plan of Action: Describe how you will improve your reading fluency during the repeated readings of your character's lines.

_____

_____

   Grades K–6 • Benchmark Advance • **Fluency** Quick Checks • © Benchmark Education Company, LLC

Reader's Theater Performance Assessment

Student: _____ Script: _____

Character I Portray: _____ Date: _____

Use the Reader's Theater Performance Assessment to record how well students performed during a Reader's Theater presentation. Information learned can be used for goal setting by students for future performances and to inform your instruction and areas in need of support.

Skill	Bravo!	Take a Bow	Star Potential	Let's Rehearse
Shows leadership while planning and rehearsing				
Works as a team member by supporting other readers				
Speaks confidently, audibly, clearly, and expressively				
Keeps audience's attention with tone, expression, and volume of voice				
Demonstrates an understanding of the character's emotions, moods, actions, and point of view				
Reads in a style that reinforces the drama or humor of the story situation				
Adjusts pitch, stress, intonation, phrasing, and pacing to achieve desired meaning				
Uses facial expressions, body language, gestures, and movement effectively				
Picks up cues without hesitation				
Listens to and reacts appropriately to other characters' lines and actions				
Stays in character even when not reading lines				
Doesn't fidget, look around, or giggle during performance				
Effectively transitions between scenes; effectively moves on- and offstage as needed				
Handles unexpected circumstances without getting ruffled				
Puts on a performance that would make the script's author smile				

Assessing Oral Presentations

Assessing oral presentations can provide opportunities to examine fluency through public speaking events. Identify how well prepared the speaker was, how well the speaker understood the subject matter, and the areas of strengths and weakness in verbal and nonverbal skills. Oral presentations provide students a forum to share understandings and build communication skills and confidence.

Grades K–6 • Benchmark Advance • **Fluency** Quick Checks • © Benchmark Education Company, LLC

Oral Presentation Rubric

Name: _____ Date: _____

Presentation Title: _____ Presentation Topic: _____ Presentation Length: _____ minutes

Presentation Element	1 (Beginning)	2 (Developing)	3 (Accomplished)	4 (Exemplary)
Content				
Subject Knowledge				
Organization				
Sources				
Delivery				
Technology, Media, Graphics, Props				
Speaking (Volume, Pacing, Word Choice, Pronunciation)				
Enthusiasm				
Eye Contact				
Body Language				
Posture & Poise				
Other				
Confidence				
Preparation				
Creativity				

Name _____ Date _____

Nan Rides the Bus

1   Nan goes to school. She rides the bus.

2   Nan gets on the bus. The bus driver says hi.

3   Nan sits in her seat. She sits with her friend.

4   The bus stops. The bus is at school!

5   Nan rides the bus home, too. She sees her mom. Her mom is at the bus stop.

6   Nan likes the big yellow bus.

Name _____ Date _____

Nan Rides the Bus

Words per Line

1   Nan goes to school. She rides   ____6
the bus.   ____8

2   Nan gets on the bus. The bus   ____15
driver says hi.   ____18

3   Nan sits in her seat.   ____23
She sits with her friend.   ____28

4   The bus stops. The bus is at school!   ____36

5   Nan rides the bus home, too.   ____42
She sees her mom.   ____46
Her mom is at the bus stop.   ____53

6   Nan likes the big yellow bus.   ____59

Comprehension Questions

1.   **What is this story mostly about?**
(riding the school bus)

2.   **With whom does Nan sit on the bus?**
(her friend)

3.   **Who is at the bus stop at the end of the story?**
(Nan's mom)

Passage	Words: 59			
Oral Reading Accuracy				%
Reading Rate				wpm
Comprehension # Correct				/3
Fluency	1	2	3	4

Name _____ Date _____

My Dog

1   My dog is big. He likes to run.
He can jump, too!

2   My dog is black.
He has big paws.
He has a long tail.

3   My dog likes to eat. He eats fast!

4   My dog sleeps in a dog bed.
The bed is in my room.

5   He is a good dog. He is my friend.

Name _____ Date _____

My Dog

Words per Line

1 My dog is big. He likes to run.	_____8
He can jump, too!	_____12
2 My dog is black.	_____16
He has big paws.	_____20
He has a long tail.	_____25
3 My dog likes to eat. He eats fast!	_____33
4 My dog sleeps in a dog bed.	_____40
The bed is in my room.	_____46
5 He is a good dog. He is my friend.	_____55

 Comprehension Questions

1. **What is this story about?**
(a dog)

2. **What color is the dog?**
(black)

3. **Where does the dog sleep?**
(in a dog bed, OR in the boy's/girl's room)

Passage	Words: 55			
Oral Reading Accuracy				%
Reading Rate				wpm
Comprehension # Correct				/3
Fluency	1	2	3	4

Name _____ Date _____

The Zoo

1   Ben goes to the zoo.
His mom and dad go, too.

2   Ben sees a lot of animals at the zoo.
He sees a fox. He sees a snake.
He sees a hippo.

3   Some of the animals are big.
The hippo is big.

4   Some of the animals are small.
The fox is small.

5   He sees an ape. He likes the ape best.

6   Ben likes going to the zoo.

Name _____ Date _____

The Zoo

	Words per Line

1   Ben goes to the zoo. ____5
His mom and dad go, too. ____11

2   Ben sees a lot of animals at the zoo. ____20
He sees a fox. He sees a snake. ____28
He sees a hippo. ____32

3   Some of the animals are big. ____38
The hippo is big. ____42

4   Some of the animals are small. ____48
The fox is small. ____52

5   He sees an ape. He likes the ape best. ____61

6   Ben likes going to the zoo. ____67

Comprehension Questions

1. **What is this story about?**
    (going to the zoo)

2. **Who goes to the zoo with Ben?**
    (his mom and dad)

3. **What animal does Ben like best?**
    (the ape)

Passage	Words: 67			
Oral Reading Accuracy				%
Reading Rate				wpm
Comprehension # Correct				/3
Fluency	1	2	3	4

Name _____ Date _____

Playing Ball

1   Tim and Jim play ball. They run and jump. They kick the ball. They have fun.

2   "Time for bed!" says Mom.

3   "Can we play more?" asks Tim.

4   "You need to sleep now," says Mom.

5   Tim and Jim go to bed.
Mom tells them a story.
It is about two boys who like to play ball.

6   Tim and Jim smile. Soon the boys are asleep.

Name _____ Date _____

Playing Ball

	Words per Line
1 Tim and Jim play ball. They run and	____8
jump. They kick the ball. They have fun.	____16
2 "Time for bed!" says Mom.	____21
3 "Can we play more?" asks Tim.	____27
4 "You need to sleep now," says Mom.	____34
5 Tim and Jim go to bed.	____40
Mom tells them a story.	____45
It is about two boys who like to play	____54
ball.	____55
6 Tim and Jim smile. Soon the boys are	____63
asleep.	____64

Comprehension Questions

1. **What do Tim and Jim like to do?**
   (play ball)

2. **Who tells Tim and Jim a story?**
   (Mom)

3. **What do Tim and Jim do at the end of the story?**
   (go to sleep)

Passage	Words: 64			
Oral Reading Accuracy				%
Reading Rate				wpm
Comprehension # Correct				/3
Fluency	1	2	3	4

Name _____ Date _____

The Moving Hat

1   Ann cannot find her cat. "Max!" Ann calls. "Where are you?" Max does not come.

2   Ann looks for Max. Then she asks Mom and Dad, "Have you seen Max?"

3   "No," say Mom and Dad.

4   Ann goes to the sunroom. Her brother Mike is there. Mike is looking at a hat on the table.

5   "What are you looking at?" Ann asks.

6   "That hat keeps moving," says Mike.

7   The hat is moving! Ann picks up the hat.

8   "Max!" says Ann. "I have been looking for you."

Name _____ Date _____

The Moving Hat

Words per Line

1   Ann cannot find her cat. "Max!" Ann   _____7
calls. "Where are you?" Max does not   _____14
come.   _____15

2   Ann looks for Max. Then she asks Mom   _____23
and Dad, "Have you seen Max?"   _____29

3   "No," say Mom and Dad.   _____34

4   Ann goes to the sunroom. Her brother   _____41
Mike is there. Mike is looking at a hat   _____50
on the table.   _____53

5   "What are you looking at?" Ann asks.   _____60

6   "That hat keeps moving," says Mike.   _____66

7   The hat is moving! Ann picks up the   _____74
hat.   _____75

8   "Max!" says Ann. "I have been looking   _____82
for you."   _____84

Comprehension Questions

1.   **What is Ann trying to do?**
(find her cat, Max)

2.   **What is Mike looking at?**
(a hat)

3.   **What does Ann do at the end of the story?**
(She finds Max under the hat.)

Passage	Words: 84			
Oral Reading Accuracy				%
Reading Rate				wpm
Comprehension # Correct				/3
Fluency	1	2	3	4

Name _____ Date _____

Bob's New Friend

1   A new boy comes to Bob's school. He likes to draw.

2   Bob says hello to the new boy. His name is Mike.

3   Bob and Mike sit together at lunch. "Do you like to play ball?" Bob says.

4   "Yes," says Mike. "Let's play!"

5   Bob and Mike go out and play ball. Mike kicks the ball. It goes into the net.

6   "Wow!" says Bob. "That was a good kick."

7   Bob is happy to have a new friend.

Name _____ Date _____

Bob's New Friend

		Words per Line
1	A new boy comes to Bob's school.	____7
	He likes to draw.	____11
2	Bob says hello to the new boy.	____18
	His name is Mike.	____22
3	Bob and Mike sit together at lunch.	____29
	"Do you like to play ball?" Bob says.	____37
4	"Yes," says Mike. "Let's play!"	____42
5	Bob and Mike go out and play ball.	____50
	Mike kicks the ball. It goes into the net.	____59
6	"Wow!" says Bob. "That was a good	____66
	kick."	____67
7	Bob is happy to have a new friend.	____75

Comprehension Questions

1. **What is this story mostly about?**
   (a new boy at school)

2. **What do Bob and Mike do first?**
   (They have lunch.)

3. **Why is Bob happy?**
   (He has a new friend.)

Passage	Words: 75			
Oral Reading Accuracy				%
Reading Rate				wpm
Comprehension # Correct				/3
Fluency	1	2	3	4

Name _____ Date _____

Stan Likes to Run

1   Stan likes to run. He runs with his dog. He runs with his dad. He runs with his friends. Stan runs all the time.

2   "I like to see you run, Stan," Mom says.

3   "I like to run," Stan says, running around Mom. "I am very fast."

4   "Do you know what time it is?" Mom asks.

5   Stan looks at the clock. He stops running and takes small, slow steps.

6   His mother smiles. It is time for bed!

Name _____ Date _____

Stan Likes to Run

		Words per Line
1	Stan likes to run. He runs with his dog.	____9
	He runs with his dad. He runs with his	____18
	friends. Stan runs all the time.	____24
2	"I like to see you run, Stan," Mom says.	____33
3	"I like to run," Stan says, running around	____41
	Mom. "I am very fast."	____46
4	"Do you know what time it is?"	____53
	Mom asks.	____55
5	Stan looks at the clock. He stops	____62
	running and takes small, slow steps.	____68
6	His mother smiles. It is time for bed!	____76

Comprehension Questions

1. **What is this story mostly about?**
   (a boy named Stan who likes to run)

2. **Whom does Stan run with?**
   (his dog, his dad, his friends)

3. **Why does Stan stop running?**
   (It is time for bed.)

Passage	Words: 76			
Oral Reading Accuracy				%
Reading Rate				wpm
Comprehension # Correct				/3
Fluency	1	2	3	4

Name _____ Date _____

Shadows

1   Kim, Ray, and Ben go to the park. They make shadows. They use their hands to make the shadows.

2   "Look at my shadow," says Kim. "Quack! It is a duck."

3   "Look at my shadow," says Ray. "Meow! It is a cat."

4   "Do you like my shadow?" asks Ben. "Woof! It is a little dog."

5   "I like your shadow," says Kim. "But who is making the shadow of a big dog?"

6   The children turn. They see Ben's dog, Duke. Duke is making the best shadow of all! The children laugh.

Name _____ Date _____

Shadows

Words per Line

1 Kim, Ray, and Ben go to the park.	_____8
They make shadows. They use their	_____14
hands to make the shadows.	_____19
2 "Look at my shadow," says Kim.	_____25
"Quack! It is a duck."	_____30
3 "Look at my shadow," says Ray. "Meow!	_____37
It is a cat."	_____41
4 "Do you like my shadow?" asks Ben.	_____48
"Woof! It is a little dog."	54
5 "I like your shadow," says Kim.	_____60
"But who is making the shadow of a	_____68
big dog?"	_____70
6 The children turn. They see Ben's dog,	_____77
Duke. Duke is making the best shadow	_____84
of all! The children laugh.	_____89

Comprehension Questions

1. **Where are Kim, Ray, and Ben?**
   (at the park)

2. **What do Kim, Ray, and Ben use to make their shadows?**
   (their hands)

3. **Why do Kim, Ray, and Ben laugh at the end of the story?**
   (They see Duke the dog making a shadow.)

Passage	Words: 89			
Oral Reading Accuracy				%
Reading Rate				wpm
Comprehension # Correct				/3
Fluency	1	2	3	4

Name _____ Date _____

Animal Homes

1 Animals live in many kinds of places. Some live in trees. Some live in the water. Some live underground.

2 Fish live in the water. They use their fins and tail to swim. They have gills to help them breathe. They may eat bugs or frogs.

3 Many birds live in trees. They make nests of grass and twigs. They eat bugs and seeds.

4 Mice live underground. They dig holes. In their homes, they can hide from bigger animals. Mice come out to find food.

Name _____ Date _____

Animal Homes

Words per Line

1   Animals live in many kinds of places.   _____7
Some live in trees. Some live in the   _____15
water. Some live underground.   _____19

2   Fish live in the water. They use their   _____27
fins and tail to swim. They have gills   _____35
to help them breathe. They may eat   _____42
bugs or frogs.   _____45

3   Many birds live in trees. They make   _____52
nests of grass and twigs. They eat bugs   _____60
and seeds.   _____ 62

4   Mice live underground. They dig   _____67
holes. In their homes, they can hide   _____74
from bigger animals. Mice come out   _____80
to find food.   _____83

Comprehension Questions

1.   **What is this passage mostly about?**
     (where animals live)

2.   **Where do birds make nests?**
     (in trees)

3.   **How do holes help mice?**
     (Holes help them hide from bigger animals, OR keep them safe.)

Passage	Words: 83			
Oral Reading Accuracy				%
Reading Rate				wpm
Comprehension # Correct				/3
Fluency	1	2	3	4

Name _____ Date _____

Jan's Day

1   Friday was Jan's birthday. "This will be a good day," said Jan. But no one said anything about her birthday.

2   At school, Jan's friends did not say anything about her birthday. "This is not such a good day," said Jan. After school, she went home.

3   When Jan got home, she called out. "Hello! Anyone?" No one answered.

4   Then she heard a yell. "Surprise! Happy birthday, Jan!" Her mom, dad, brother, and friends from school were all there.

5   "You did not forget my birthday," said Jan.

6   "We wanted to surprise you," her mom said.

7   Jan grinned. "It is a good day after all!"

Name _____ Date _____

Jan's Day

Words per Line

1   Friday was Jan's birthday. "This will be   ____7
a good day," said Jan. But no one said   ____16
anything about her birthday.   ____20

2   At school, Jan's friends did not say   ____27
anything about her birthday. "This is not   ____34
such a good day," said Jan. After school,   ____42
she went home.   ____45

3   When Jan got home, she called out.   ____52
"Hello! Anyone?" No one answered.   ____57

4   Then she heard a yell. "Surprise! Happy   ____64
birthday, Jan!" Her mom, dad, brother,   ____70
and friends from school were all there.   ____77

5   "You did not forget my birthday,"   ____83
said Jan.   ____85

6   "We wanted to surprise you," her mom   ____92
said.   ____93

7   Jan grinned. "It is a good day after all!"   ____102

Comprehension Questions

1. **What is this story mostly about?**
   (Jan's birthday, OR a surprise party)

2. **Why was Jan sad at the beginning of the story?**
   (No one wished her a happy birthday.)

3. **What happened when Jan got home from school?**
   (Her friends and family had a party for her.)

Passage	Words: 102			
Oral Reading Accuracy				%
Reading Rate				wpm
Comprehension # Correct				/3
Fluency	1	2	3	4

Name _____ Date _____

All About Me

1   Lee's father sat in a big chair. He was reading a book and smiling.

2   "What are you reading?" Lee asked.

3   "I'm reading a book about a special person," said Lee's father.

4   Lee looked at the book. "It has pictures of a baby," she said. "That baby is cute!"

5   Lee's father said, "That baby is smart, too. That baby could say lots of words before age two. That baby even learned to walk all by herself."

6   "Who is that cute, smart baby?" Lee asked.

7   "It's you!" Lee's father said with a laugh.

Name _____ Date _____

All About Me

Words per Line

1   Lee's father sat in a big chair. He was
reading a book and smiling.

_____9
_____14

2   "What are you reading?" Lee asked.

_____20

3   "I'm reading a book about a special
person," said Lee's father.

_____27
_____31

4   Lee looked at the book. "It has pictures
of a baby," she said. "That baby is cute!"

_____39
_____48

5   Lee's father said, "That baby is smart,
too. That baby could say lots of words
before age two. That baby even learned
to walk all by herself."

_____55
_____63
_____70
_____75

6   "Who is that cute, smart baby?"
Lee asked.

_____81
_____83

7   "It's you!" Lee's father said with a laugh.

_____91

Comprehension Questions

1.   What is Lee's father doing at the beginning of the story?
(reading a book)

2.   What does Lee see in the book?
(pictures of a baby)

3.   Why does Lee's father laugh?
(The book is about Lee.)

Passage	Words: 91			
Oral Reading Accuracy				%
Reading Rate				wpm
Comprehension # Correct				/3
Fluency	1	2	3	4

Name _____ Date _____

Max's Job

1   Max lives in a place that gets lots of snow. All the neighbors hire Max to shovel their snow.

2   One day, Max looked out the window. No snow! "When will we have snow, Mom?" Max asked. "I can't do my job!"

3   "You could walk dogs instead of shoveling snow," said Mom.

4   "No, thanks!" said Max.

5   "You could be a paperboy," suggested Dad.

6   "No, thanks!" said Max.

7   Thinking about snow made Max look outside. "Come on, SNOW!" he said to the sky. Suddenly, a snowflake floated by the window, then another, then another.

8   "Yay!" said Max. "I can do my job again."

Name _____ Date _____

Max's Job

		Words per Line
1	Max lives in a place that gets lots	_____8
	of snow. All the neighbors hire Max to	_____16
	shovel their snow.	_____19
2	One day, Max looked out the window.	_____26
	No snow! "When will we have snow,	_____33
	Mom?" Max asked. "I can't do my job!"	_____41
3	"You could walk dogs instead of	_____47
	shoveling snow," said Mom.	_____51
4	"No, thanks!" said Max.	_____55
5	"You could be a paperboy,"	_____60
	suggested Dad.	_____62
6	"No, thanks!" said Max.	_____66
7	Thinking about snow made Max look	_____72
	outside. "Come on...SNOW!" he said to	_____79
	the sky. Suddenly, a snowflake floated by	_____86
	the window, then another, then another.	_____92
8	"Yay!" said Max. "I can do my job	_____100
	again."	_____101

Comprehension Questions

1. **What is Max's job?**
   (shoveling snow)

2. **What jobs do Mom and Dad suggest?**
   (walking dogs, paperboy)

3. **How does Max feel at the end of the story? Tell why.**
   (He is happy because it is snowing and he can do his job.)

Passage	Words: 101			
Oral Reading Accuracy				%
Reading Rate				wpm
Comprehension # Correct				/3
Fluency	1	2	3	4

Name _____ Date _____

Roy Earns Money

1   Roy lives on a farm. He helps his mom and dad. He does many chores. He feeds the animals. Roy has his own small patch of corn, too.

2   Roy's best friend is Tug. "Let's join the after-school art club this fall," says Tug. "It costs only ten dollars."

3   "I don't have ten dollars," says Roy. Then he grins. "But I can sell some corn! I can make ten dollars."

4   Roy tells his mom and dad about his plan. "That's a good idea," says Mom.

5   "You can sell corn to people who drive by the farm," says Dad.

6   Roy picks his corn. He sets up a stand in front of the farm. People stop and buy corn. Soon, Roy has the money he needs for the art club.

Grades K–6 • Benchmark Advance • **Fluency** Quick Checks • © Benchmark Education Company, LLC

Name _____ Date _____

Roy Earns Money

Words per Line

1   Roy lives on a farm. He helps his mom   _____9
     and dad. He does many chores. He   _____16
     feeds the animals. Roy has his own small   _____24
     patch of corn, too.   _____28

2   Roy's best friend is Tug. "Let's join the   _____36
     after-school art club this fall," says Tug.   _____43
     "It costs only ten dollars."   _____48

3   "I don't have ten dollars," says Roy.   _____55
     Then he grins. "But I can sell some corn!   _____64
     I can make ten dollars."   _____69

4   Roy tells his mom and dad about his   _____77
     plan. "That's a good idea," says Mom.   _____84

5   "You can sell corn to people who drive   _____92
     by the farm," says Dad.   _____97

6   Roy picks his corn. He sets up a stand   _____106
     in front of the farm. People stop and   _____114
     buy corn. Soon, Roy has the money he   _____122
     needs for the art club.   _____127

Comprehension Questions

1.   **Where does Roy live?**
     (on a farm)

2.   **What is Roy's problem in the story?**
     (He does not have money to sign up for the art club.)

3.   **What does Roy do to earn money?**
     (He sells corn.)

Passage	Words: 127			
Oral Reading Accuracy				%
Reading Rate				wpm
Comprehension # Correct				/3
Fluency	1	2	3	4

Name _____ Date _____

The Walking Bus

1 Ten children at Park Lane School go home in the walking bus. The bus leaves the school at the end of the day.

2 Mrs. Green walks in front of the bus. Mr. Scott walks in back of the bus. The children walk in the middle.

3 "Here we go!" says Mrs. Green as the bus starts to move. "Look out for cars."

4 The bus goes slowly. It stops at Ben's house. It stops at Maria's house. It stops eight more times until all the children are home! Then the bus's job is done.

Name _____   Date _____

The Walking Bus

		Words per Line
1	Ten children at Park Lane School	____6
	go home in the walking bus.	____12
	The bus leaves the school at the	____19
	end of the day.	____23
2	Mrs. Green walks in front of the bus.	____31
	Mr. Scott walks in back of the bus.	____39
	The children walk in the middle.	____45
3	"Here we go!" says Mrs. Green as the	____53
	bus starts to move. "Look out for cars."	____61
4	The bus goes slowly. It stops at Ben's	____69
	house. It stops at Maria's house. It stops	____77
	eight more times until all the children	____84
	are home! Then the bus's job is done.	____92

Comprehension Questions

1. **What does a walking bus do?**
   (A walking bus takes children home from school.)

2. **Who walks in front of the walking bus?**
   (Mrs. Green, OR a teacher)

3. **Where does the walking bus stop?**
   (The walking bus stops at each child's house.)

Passage	Words: 92			
Oral Reading Accuracy				%
Reading Rate				wpm
Comprehension # Correct				/3
Fluency	1	2	3	4

Name _____ Date _____

Snow Days

1   Many people like snow. On snow days, there is no school. Kids like to sled. They build snowmen. They make snowballs.

2   Some people work to get rid of the snow. They drive big trucks with plows. The plows push the snow out of the road. These drivers help people.

3   Snow days are hard for some people. Mail carriers have to bring the mail. They must work, even in a big snowstorm. It is hard to walk in deep snow. People who build houses or fix roads cannot work in the snow. The snow gets in their way.

Name _____ Date _____

Snow Days

Words per Line

1   Many people like snow. On snow
days, there is no school. Kids like to
sled. They build snowmen. They make
snowballs.

_____6
_____14
_____20
_____21

2   Some people work to get rid of the
snow. They drive big trucks with plows.
The plows push the snow out of the
road. These drivers help people.

_____29
_____36
_____44
_____49

3   Snow days are hard for some
people. Mail carriers have to bring the
mail. They must work, even in a big
snowstorm. It is hard to walk in deep
snow. People who build houses or fix
roads cannot work in the snow. The
snow gets in their way.

_____55
_____62
_____70
_____78
_____85
_____92
_____97

Comprehension Questions

1.   **What happens at school on snow days?**
(There is no school, OR the school closes.)

2.   **What does a snow plow do?**
(moves snow out of the road)

3.   **Why don't mail carriers like snow days?**
(Snow makes their job hard, OR it's hard to walk in deep snow.)

Passage	Words: 97			
Oral Reading Accuracy				%
Reading Rate				wpm
Comprehension # Correct				/3
Fluency	1	2	3	4

Name _____ Date _____

Insects

1   Our world has more than one million kinds of insects. Insects fall into two main groups. Some insects have wings. Beetles and house flies are insects. They have wings. Other insects do not have wings.

2   Insects do not have a backbone. They do not have bones at all. Instead, they have a hard outer covering.

3   Every insect's body has three parts. And all insects have six legs. Bees and ants are insects. They have six legs. Spiders are not insects because they have eight legs. Other bugs have even more legs. Centipedes have hundreds of legs! They are not insects, either.

4   Insects make up more than 90 percent of living things in the world. That's a lot of insects!

Name _____ Date _____

Insects

Words per Line

1   Our world has more than one million kinds   _____8
of insects. Insects fall into two main groups.   _____16
Some insects have wings. Beetles and house   _____23
flies are insects. They have wings. Other insects   _____31
do not have wings.   _____35

2   Insects do not have a backbone. They do   _____43
not have bones at all. Instead, they have a   _____52
hard outer covering.   _____55

3   Every insect's body has three parts. And   _____62
all insects have six legs. Bees and ants are   _____71
insects. They have six legs. Spiders are not   _____79
insects because they have eight legs. Other   _____86
bugs have even more legs. Centipedes have   _____93
hundreds of legs! They are not insects, either.   _____101

4   Insects make up more than 90 percent   _____108
of living things in the world. That's a lot of   _____118
insects!   _____119

Comprehension Questions

1.   **What things do all insects have?**
(six legs, OR three body parts, OR hard outer covering)

2.   **What are the two main groups of insects?**
(insects with wings and insects without wings)

3.   **Why aren't centipedes called insects?**
(They have more than six legs.)

Passage	Words: 119			
Oral Reading Accuracy				%
Reading Rate				wpm
Comprehension # Correct				/3
Fluency	1	2	3	4

Name _____ Date _____

The Painting

1   Matt likes to paint. Matt paints pictures of things he sees outside, like cars and trees.

2   Meg is Matt's little sister. Meg watches Matt paint. "I want to paint, too," says Meg. "What can I paint?"

3   Matt gets a big piece of paper. Matt puts the paper on the table. He gets some finger paints for Meg. He puts the finger paints on the table.

4   "Now we can paint a picture together," says Matt.

5   Meg paints first. She uses her hands. She makes green lines on the paper.

6   "I see grass outside," says Meg.

7   Then Matt paints. Matt uses a brush. He paints a flower in the grass.

Name _____ Date _____

The Painting

Words per Line

1   Matt likes to paint. Matt paints pictures of
things he sees outside, like cars and trees.

_____8
_____16

2   Meg is Matt's little sister. Meg watches Matt
paint. "I want to paint, too," says Meg.
"What can I paint?"

_____24
_____32
_____36

3   Matt gets a big piece of paper. Matt puts
the paper on the table. He gets some finger
paints for Meg. He puts the finger paints on
the table.

_____45
_____54
_____63
_____65

4   "Now we can paint a picture together,"
says Matt.

_____72
_____74

5   Meg paints first. She uses her hands. She
makes green lines on the paper.

_____82
_____88

6   "I see grass outside," says Meg.

_____94

7   Then Matt paints. Matt uses a brush.
He paints a flower in the grass.

_____101
_____108

Comprehension Questions

1. **What do Matt and Meg both like to do?**
   (paint pictures)

2. **What does Matt do for Meg?**
   (He gets paper and finger paints for her.)

3. **What do Matt and Meg paint?**
   (grass and a flower)

Passage	Words: 108			
Oral Reading Accuracy				%
Reading Rate				wpm
Comprehension # Correct				/3
Fluency	1	2	3	4

Name _____ Date _____

Growing Plants

1   A plant starts out as a seed. Plants need air, water, and sunlight to grow.

2   First, you have to put the seed in some soil. Then give it some water. Water helps it grow. It also needs heat from the sun.

3   Soon, a little green sprout shoots out of the soil. The plant is coming up!

4   A plant has roots in the ground. You can't see them, but they have an important job. They drink up water from the soil. This helps the plant grow bigger.

5   The sun helps the plant grow, too. A plant uses air and sunlight to make its own food.

Name _____ Date _____

Growing Plants

Words per Line

1   A plant starts out as a seed. Plants need air,   ____10
water, and sunlight to grow.   ____15

2   First, you have to put the seed in some soil.   ____25
Then give it some water. Water helps it grow.   ____34
It also needs heat from the sun.   ____41

3   Soon, a little green sprout shoots out of the   ____50
soil. The plant is coming up!   ____56

4   A plant has roots in the ground. You can't   ____65
see them, but they have an important job.   ____73
They drink up water from the soil. This helps   ____82
the plant grow bigger.   ____86

5   The sun helps the plant grow, too. A plant   ____95
uses air and sunlight to make its own food.   ____104

Comprehension Questions

1. **What is this passage mostly about?**
    (what plants need to grow, OR how plants grow)

2. **How do the roots help the plant?**
    (They drink up water from the soil.)

3. **What does the plant need to make its own food?**
    (air and sunlight)

Passage	Words: 104			
Oral Reading Accuracy				%
Reading Rate				wpm
Comprehension # Correct				/3
Fluency	1	2	3	4

Name _____ Date _____

Bird Rescue

1   Mom and I were in the yard. I saw a baby blue jay fall out of its nest. It landed on the grass. Then I saw Tabby, our cat! Tabby walked slowly toward the bird.

2   "Mom! Tabby is going to get the baby bird!" I cried.

3   Mom said, "Oh, no! I will get Tabby."

4   Next, a big blue jay flew over Tabby's head. It landed in the grass. Tabby ran toward the big bird. Then the big blue jay flew away.

5   Tabby looked back at the baby bird. We looked, too. The baby bird flapped its tiny wings and flew away. The big blue jay waited for the baby bird in the nest.

6   The baby bird did not need our help after all.

Grades K–6 • Benchmark Advance • **Fluency** Quick Checks • © Benchmark Education Company, LLC

Name _____ Date _____

Bird Rescue

Words per Line

1   Mom and I were in the yard. I saw a baby   _____11
blue jay fall out of its nest. It landed on   _____21
the grass. Then I saw Tabby, our cat! Tabby   _____30
walked slowly toward the bird.   _____35

2   "Mom! Tabby is going to get the baby bird!"   _____44
I cried.   _____46

3   Mom said, "Oh, no! I will get Tabby."   _____54

4   Next, a big blue jay flew over Tabby's head.   _____63
It landed in the grass. Tabby ran toward the   _____72
big bird. Then the big blue jay flew away.   _____81

5   Tabby looked back at the baby bird. We   _____89
looked, too. The baby bird flapped its tiny   _____97
wings and flew away. The big blue jay   _____105
waited for the baby bird in the nest.   _____113

6   The baby bird did not need our help   _____121
after all.   _____123

Comprehension Questions

1. **Where did the baby bird come from?**
(a nest)

2. **Why is the child worried about Tabby?**
(He/she doesn't want Tabby to get the baby bird.)

3. **What happens at the end of the story?**
(The baby bird flies back to the nest.)

Passage	Words: 123			
Oral Reading Accuracy				**%**
Reading Rate				**wpm**
Comprehension # Correct				**/3**
Fluency	**1**	**2**	**3**	**4**

Name _____ Date _____

Kim's Bad Day

1   Kim had a bad day. First, her brother ate the last bowl of Silly Shapes cereal. Kim had to eat her mother's wheat flakes. Then Kim missed the bus. She had to get a ride from her dad.

2   Ms. Lopez gave the class a spelling quiz. Kim looked at the quiz and frowned. She had studied the wrong list of words! Ms. Lopez drew a sad face on Kim's paper.

3   Kim went home and showed her mother the spelling quiz. Mom made a sad face like the one Ms. Lopez drew on the paper.

4   Kim walked slowly to her room. Then she bumped into something big and furry. It was her dog, Buddy. Kim showed Buddy the quiz. Buddy did not frown. Buddy tried to eat the paper! Kim laughed and hugged her dog.

Name _____ Date _____

Kim's Bad Day

	Words per Line

1   Kim had a bad day. First, her brother ate   ____9
the last bowl of Silly Shapes cereal. Kim had   ____18
to eat her mother's wheat flakes. Then Kim   ____26
missed the bus. She had to get a ride from   ____36
her dad.   ____38

2   Ms. Lopez gave the class a spelling quiz.   ____46
Kim looked at the quiz and frowned. She had   ____55
studied the wrong list of words! Ms. Lopez   ____63
drew a sad face on Kim's paper.   ____70

3   Kim went home and showed her mother the   78
spelling quiz. Mom made a sad face like the   ____87
one Ms. Lopez drew on the paper.   94

4   Kim walked slowly to her room. Then she   ____102
bumped into something big and furry. It was   ____110
her dog, Buddy. Kim showed Buddy the quiz.   ____118
Buddy did not frown. Buddy tried to eat the   ____127
paper! Kim laughed and hugged her dog.   ____134

Comprehension Questions

1. **Why does Kim have a bad day? Give at least two reasons.**
    (Her brother ate the cereal. She missed the bus. She did poorly on a spelling test.)

2. **How does Kim get to school in the story?**
    (Her dad gives her a ride.)

3. **Why does Kim do poorly on the spelling quiz?**
    (She studied the wrong words.)

Passage	Words: 134			
Oral Reading Accuracy				%
Reading Rate				wpm
Comprehension # Correct				/3
Fluency	1	2	3	4

Name _____ Date _____

Lost and Found

1   As Liz was walking home one day, she saw something on the sidewalk. It was a diamond ring! Liz picked it up and put it on her finger.

2   When Liz got home, she showed the ring to her mother. "I found it on the sidewalk," said Liz.

3   "Someone lost that ring. It is valuable," said Mother.

4   Liz wanted to keep the ring. But she knew what she should do. Liz took the ring to the police station.

5   "A woman just called about this ring," said the officer. "The ring is very special to her. Thank you for bringing it in."

6   A few days later, Liz got a letter from the police officer. It said, "The owner of the ring has left you a reward. You may pick up the reward at the station."

7   "It pays to do the right thing," said Liz.

Name _____ Date _____

Lost and Found

Words per Line

1   As Liz was walking home one day, she saw
something on the sidewalk. It was a diamond
ring! Liz picked it up and put it on her finger.

_____9
_____17
_____28

2   When Liz got home, she showed the ring to
her mother. "I found it on the sidewalk,"
said Liz.

_____37
_____45
_____47

3   "Someone lost that ring. It is valuable,"
said Mother.

_____54
_____56

4   Liz wanted to keep the ring. But she knew
what she should do. Liz took the ring to the
police station.

_____65
_____75
_____77

5   "A woman just called about this ring," said
the officer. "The ring is very special to her.
Thank you for bringing it in."

_____85
_____94
_____100

6   A few days later, Liz got a letter from the
police officer. It said, "The owner of the ring
has left you a reward. You may pick up the
reward at the station."

_____110
_____119
_____129
_____133

7   "It pays to do the right thing," said Liz.

_____142

Comprehension Questions

1.   **What was Liz doing when she found the ring?**
     (She was walking home.)

2.   **Why did Liz decide to return the ring?**
     (She knew it was the right thing to do.)

3.   **What did the ring's owner do for Liz?**
     (She gave Liz a reward.)

Passage	Words: 142			
Oral Reading Accuracy				%
Reading Rate				wpm
Comprehension # Correct				/3
Fluency	1	2	3	4

Name _____ Date _____

Clouds

1   Look up in the sky. You may see many types of clouds.

2   A cloud is a group of tiny ice crystals or water droplets. When billions of these droplets or crystals come together, they form a cloud. Clouds are very light, so they float in the air.

3   The wind moves clouds along in the sky. If it is a windy day, you'll see the clouds move very fast. On calm days, the clouds hardly seem to move at all.

4   Clouds form at different heights in the sky: high, middle, and low. Cirrus clouds are high clouds. They look thin and long, like streamers. Cirrus clouds are fair-weather clouds. They don't make rain. Stratus clouds are low clouds. They are usually gray and cover up the whole sky. Rain can fall from these clouds.

Name _____ Date _____

Clouds

Words per Line

1   Look up in the sky. You may see many types _____10
of clouds. _____12

2   A cloud is a group of tiny ice crystals or _____22
water droplets. When billions of these droplets _____29
or crystals come together, they form a cloud. _____37
Clouds are very light, so they float in the air. _____47

3   The wind moves clouds along in the sky. If _____56
it is a windy day, you'll see the clouds move _____66
very fast. On calm days, the clouds hardly _____74
seem to move at all. _____79

4   Clouds form at different heights in the sky: _____87
high, middle, and low. Cirrus clouds are high _____95
clouds. They look thin and long, like streamers. _____103
Cirrus clouds are fair-weather clouds. They _____109
don't make rain. Stratus clouds are low clouds. _____117
They are usually gray and cover up the whole _____126
sky. Rain can fall from these clouds. _____133

Comprehension Questions

1.   **What is this passage mostly about?**
       (different kinds of clouds)

2.   **Why are cirrus clouds called "fair-weather clouds"?**
       (They don't make rain.)

3.   **What are low clouds like?**
       (They are gray. They cover the sky. They bring rain.)

Passage	Words: 133			
Oral Reading Accuracy				%
Reading Rate				wpm
Comprehension # Correct				/3
Fluency	1	2	3	4

Name _____ Date _____

Warm and Cool Forests

1   Warm and cool places have different
kinds of forests. In warmer places, you
see woodland forests. Colder places have
mountain forests.

2   Woodland forests have mostly leafy trees.
These include oak, elm, beech, and many
other kinds. The leaves on these trees are
big and wide. They turn colors in the fall.
Then the leaves fall off. The trees stay bare
until the spring.

3   Mountain forests have pine trees, fir trees,
and spruce trees. These kinds of trees do
not really have leaves. Instead, they have
needles. These needles stay green all year
long. They do not fall off. These types of trees
are called "evergreens."

4   Some warm forests have evergreen trees,
too. But cold forests do not have leafy trees.
The air is too cold for these trees to live up
high on the mountains.

Name _____ Date _____

Warm and Cool Forests

Words per Line

1   Warm and cool places have different   ____6
kinds of forests. In warmer places, you   ____13
see woodland forests. Colder places have   ____19
mountain forests.   ____21

2   Woodland forests have mostly leafy trees.   ____27
These include oak, elm, beech, and many   ____34
other kinds. The leaves on these trees are   ____42
big and wide. They turn colors in the fall.   ____51
Then the leaves fall off. The trees stay bare   ____60
until the spring.   ____63

3   Mountain forests have pine trees, fir trees, ____70
and spruce trees. These kinds of trees do   ____78
not really have leaves. Instead, they have   ____85
needles. These needles stay green all year   ____92
long. They do not fall off. These types of trees ____102
are called "evergreens."   ____105

4   Some warm forests have evergreen trees,   ____111
too. But cold forests do not have leafy trees.   ____120
The air is too cold for these trees to live up   ____131
high on the mountains.   ____135

Comprehension Questions

1. **What is this passage mostly about?**
    (different kinds of forests, OR woodland forests and mountain forests)

2. **How are leafy trees different from evergreens?**
    (The leaves of leafy trees turn color and fall off.)

3. **Why can't oak and beech trees live up high in the mountains?**
    (It is too cold.)

Passage	Words: 135			
Oral Reading Accuracy				%
Reading Rate				wpm
Comprehension # Correct				/3
Fluency	1	2	3	4

Name _____ Date _____

TV History

1   Before the TV was invented, people listened to the radio to get their news. They also listened to funny and interesting radio shows.

2   Today, most people have TVs in their homes. Many people have cable TV. They get hundreds of channels! The picture on the TV is very clear and in color.

3   When TV was first made, it was very different. First, the images were in black and white. The images were not as clear as they are today. And there were only a few channels to watch.

4   The first TV was made in the late 1920s. But people did not buy many TVs until the 1940s. By 1954, a little more than half of the homes in the United States had TVs.

5   People were very excited about TV. Some families who owned a TV had "viewing parties." They invited their friends and family over to watch special shows.

Name _____   Date _____

TV History

Words per Line

1   Before the TV was invented, people listened   ____7
to the radio to get their news. They also   ____16
listened to funny and interesting radio shows.   ____23

2   Today, most people have TVs in their homes.   ____31
Many people have cable TV. They get   ____38
hundreds of channels! The picture on the TV   ____46
is very clear and in color.   ____52

3   When TV was first made, it was very   ____60
different. First, the images were in black   ____67
and white. The images were not as clear as   ____76
they are today. And there were only a few   ____85
channels to watch.   ____88

4   The first TV was made in the late 1920s. But   ____98
people did not buy many TVs until the 1940s.   ____107
By 1954, a little more than half of the homes   ____117
in the United States had TVs.   ____123

5   People were very excited about TV. Some   ____130
families who owned a TV had "viewing   ____137
parties." They invited their friends and family   ____144
over to watch special shows.   ____149

Comprehension Questions

1.   **What is one way TVs today are different from the first TVs ever made?**
     (TVs today are in color OR are clearer OR get many channels.)

2.   **Why did people have TV viewing parties?**
     (so their friends and family without TVs could watch shows, too)

3.   **How did people learn about the news before TVs?**
     (They listened to the radio.)

Passage	Words: 149			
Oral Reading Accuracy				%
Reading Rate				wpm
Comprehension # Correct				/3
Fluency	1	2	3	4

Name _____ Date _____

Squanto

1   On March 22, 1621, a man named Squanto met with the Pilgrims. The Pilgrims had sailed from England a few months earlier on a ship called the *Mayflower*. The Pilgrims landed in America and started a town.

2   Squanto was a Native American, but he spoke English. The Pilgrims needed Squanto's help. They barely lived through the first winter. They were cold. They were hungry.

3   Squanto stayed with the Pilgrims. He showed them how to build warm homes. He showed them how to plant corn. Squanto also showed the Pilgrims where to fish and how to find nuts and berries.

4   Without Squanto's help, the Pilgrims might not have made it through another winter.

Grades K–6 • Benchmark Advance • **Fluency** Quick Checks • © Benchmark Education Company, LLC

Name _____ Date _____

Squanto

Words per Line

1   On March 22, 1621, a man named Squanto met with the Pilgrims. The Pilgrims had sailed from England a few months earlier on a ship called the *Mayflower.* The Pilgrims landed in America and started a town.

_____8
_____16
_____25
_____32
_____37

2   Squanto was a Native American, but he spoke English. The Pilgrims needed Squanto's help. They barely lived through the first winter. They were cold. They were hungry.

_____44
_____50
_____58
_____64

3   Squanto stayed with the Pilgrims. He showed them how to build warm homes. He showed them how to plant corn. Squanto also showed the Pilgrims where to fish and how to find nuts and berries.

_____71
_____79
_____87
_____97
_____99

4   Without Squanto's help, the Pilgrims might not have made it through another winter.

_____106
_____112

Comprehension Questions

1.   **What is this passage mostly about?**
     (how Squanto helped the Pilgrims)

2.   **Why did the Pilgrims need help?**
     (They did not have enough food. They were cold.)

3.   **How did Squanto help the Pilgrims?**
     (He helped them build warm homes. He showed them how to grow and find food.)

Passage	Words: 112			
Oral Reading Accuracy				**%**
Reading Rate				**wpm**
Comprehension # Correct				**/3**
Fluency	**1**	**2**	**3**	**4**

Name _____ Date _____

Mouse's Escape

1   One morning, Mouse fell into a large hole in the woods. It was a trap dug by hunters, and Mouse could not hop out. He was upset.

2   Soon Elephant came along. Mouse pleaded with Elephant to help him. Elephant stretched his trunk into the hole. But Mouse could not reach it. Mouse became angry. He scolded Elephant for not helping him.

3   "You've hurt my feelings, so I'm leaving," said Elephant.

4   "Forgive me, my wise and kind friend," said Mouse quickly. "There must be a way out of this trap. If you climb down here with me, we can think of it together."

5   Soothed by Mouse's words, Elephant climbed down into the hole. As soon as Elephant reached the bottom, Mouse scurried up his leg. Then he hopped onto his back. From there, he leaped out of the hole and ran off, leaving Elephant behind.

Name _____ Date _____

Mouse's Escape

Words per Line

1   One morning, Mouse fell into a large hole in the   _____10
woods. It was a trap dug by hunters, and Mouse could   _____21
not hop out. He was upset.   _____27

2   Soon Elephant came along. Mouse pleaded with   _____34
Elephant to help him. Elephant stretched his trunk into   _____43
the hole. But Mouse could not reach it. Mouse became   _____53
angry. He scolded Elephant for not helping him.   _____61

3   "You've hurt my feelings, so I'm leaving," said Elephant.   _____70

4   "Forgive me, my wise and kind friend," said Mouse   _____79
quickly. "There must be a way out of this trap. If you   _____91
climb down here with me, we can think of it together."   _____102

5   Soothed by Mouse's words, Elephant climbed down into   _____110
the hole. As soon as Elephant reached the bottom, Mouse   _____120
scurried up his leg. Then he hopped onto his back. From   _____131
there, he leaped out of the hole and ran off, leaving   _____142
Elephant behind.   _____144

Comprehension Questions

1.   **What happened to Mouse at the beginning of the story?**
      (He fell into a deep hole/a trap.)

2.   **Why did Mouse become angry with Elephant?**
      (He couldn't reach the elephant's trunk, so he got mad.)

3.   **How did Mouse get out of the hole?**
      (He got Elephant to come down into the hole. Then he climbed up Elephant to get out.)

Passage	Words: 144			
Oral Reading Accuracy				%
Reading Rate				wpm
Comprehension # Correct				/3
Fluency	1	2	3	4

Name _____ Date _____

Rabbit's Feast

1   One day, Rabbit went down to the river for a drink of water. Then he spotted a large berry bush on the other side of the river.

2   Just then, Rabbit noticed Crocodile swimming toward him. Crocodile wanted to eat Rabbit as much as Rabbit wanted to eat the berries. Rabbit knew he had to think fast.

3   "I have good news, Crocodile!" Rabbit began. "The forest animals are holding a feast. The crocodiles are invited! I've come to count all the crocodiles. We want to make sure we have enough food for you."

4   Crocodile was delighted. He smacked his tail on the water to call his friends. Rabbit told them all to line up so he could count them. When the crocodiles lined up, they formed a bridge across the water.

5   "Now I will count," Rabbit declared. With that, he hopped across the crocodiles' backs, counting as he went. When Rabbit reached the other side, he rushed off to eat the berries.

Name _____ Date _____

Rabbit's Feast

Words per Line

1   One day, Rabbit went down to the river for a drink   _____11
of water. Then he spotted a large berry bush on the   _____22
other side of the river.   _____27

2   Just then, Rabbit noticed Crocodile swimming toward   _____34
him. Crocodile wanted to eat Rabbit as much as   _____43
Rabbit wanted to eat the berries. Rabbit knew he had   _____53
to think fast.   _____56

3   "I have good news, Crocodile!" Rabbit began. "The   _____64
forest animals are holding a feast. The crocodiles are   _____73
invited! I've come to count all the crocodiles. We want   _____83
to make sure we have enough food for you."   _____92

4   Crocodile was delighted. He smacked his tail on the   _____101
water to call his friends. Rabbit told them all to line   _____112
up so he could count them. When the crocodiles lined   _____122
up, they formed a bridge across the water.   _____130

5   "Now I will count," Rabbit declared. With that, he   _____139
hopped across the crocodiles' backs, counting as he   _____147
went. When Rabbit reached the other side, he rushed   _____156
off to eat the berries.   _____161

Comprehension Questions

1. **Why did Rabbit go down to the river?**
    (to get a drink of water)

2. **What was Rabbit's problem?**
    (He could not get to the berry bush across the river.)

3. **How did Rabbit trick the crocodiles?**
    (He told them there was a feast and he needed to count them to make sure there was enough food. Then he hopped over the crocodiles' backs.)

Passage	Words: 161			
Oral Reading Accuracy				%
Reading Rate				wpm
Comprehension # Correct				/3
Fluency	1	2	3	4

Name _____ Date _____

Now THAT's a Pumpkin!

1   Every fall, thousands of people travel to Half Moon Bay, California. They go to see a pumpkin-growing contest. It is called the World Championship Pumpkin Weigh-Off. Farmers bring pumpkins from all over the country. They compete to see who grew the biggest one. Winners take home prizes and money.

2   The first contest took place in 1974. The winning pumpkin weighed a little more than one hundred pounds. After that, the pumpkins got bigger every year. Now, growers bring their pumpkins in on trucks. Then a forklift picks up each pumpkin and places it on a scale.

3   In 2012, the world's biggest pumpkin weighed just over a ton. Today's world record is 2,323 pounds. It was set in Germany in 2014.

4   In the 2015 contest, first place went to Steve Daletas from Oregon. But his pumpkin was not orange! He grew a cream-colored pumpkin. It was the size of a small car and weighed almost a ton.

Grades K–6 • Benchmark Advance • **Fluency** Quick Checks • © Benchmark Education Company, LLC

Name _____ Date _____

Now THAT's a Pumpkin!

Words per Line

1   Every fall, thousands of people travel to Half Moon Bay, California. They go to see a pumpkin growing contest. It is called the World Championship Pumpkin Weigh-Off. Farmers bring pumpkins from all over the country. They compete to see who grew the biggest one. Winners take home prizes and money.

_____10
_____19
_____27
_____36
_____46
_____50

2   The first contest took place in 1974. The winning pumpkin weighed a little more than one hundred pounds. After that, the pumpkins got bigger every year. Now, growers bring their pumpkins in on trucks. Then a forklift picks up each pumpkin and places it on a scale.

_____59
_____68
_____77
_____87
_____97

3   In 2012, the world's biggest pumpkin weighed just over a ton. Today's world record is 2,323 pounds. It was set in Germany in 2014.

_____106
_____117
_____121

4   In the 2015 contest, first place went to Steve Daletas from Oregon. But his pumpkin was not orange! He grew a cream-colored pumpkin. It was the size of a small car and weighed almost a ton.

_____131
_____141
_____152
_____157

Comprehension Questions

1.   **What is this passage mostly about?**
     (a pumpkin-growing contest)

2.   **How do growers weigh their pumpkins at the contest?**
     (They bring the pumpkins in on trucks, and a forklift places each pumpkin on a scale.)

3.   **What was unusual about the prize-winning pumpkin in 2015?**
     (It was cream-colored, OR it was the size of a small car.)

Passage	Words: 157			
Oral Reading Accuracy				%
Reading Rate				wpm
Comprehension # Correct				/3
Fluency	1	2	3	4

Name _____ Date _____

Kate's Trip

1   "I'm so excited to be in New York City!" said Kate.

2   Kate and her family got on the elevator. They were on their way to the top of the Empire State Building. The building was once the tallest in New York City. It was even the tallest building in the world at one time.

3   When the elevator reached the top, Kate and her family filed out. Even though the day was chilly, they went outside on the deck to enjoy the view.

4   Kate did not know where to look first. She couldn't believe how small some of the other buildings looked from this height. Houses, cars, and trees looked tiny.

5   To the south, she saw the Brooklyn Bridge. To the north was a big green space she knew was Central Park.

6   Kate took out her camera and started taking pictures. She couldn't wait to share them with her classmates back home.

Name _____ Date _____

Kate's Trip

Words per Line

1   "I'm so excited to be in New York City!" said Kate.   ____11

2   Kate and her family got on the elevator. They were on   ____22
their way to the top of the Empire State Building. The   ____33
building was once the tallest in New York City. It was   ____44
even the tallest building in the world at one time.   ____54

3   When the elevator reached the top, Kate and her   ____63
family filed out. Even though the day was chilly, they   ____73
went outside on the deck to enjoy the view.   ____82

4   Kate did not know where to look first. She couldn't   ____92
believe how small some of the other buildings looked   ____101
from this height. Houses, cars, and trees looked tiny.   ____110

5   To the south, she saw the Brooklyn Bridge. To the   ____120
north was a big green space she knew was Central Park.   ____131

6   Kate took out her camera and started taking pictures.   ____140
She couldn't wait to share them with her classmates   ____149
back home.   ____151

Comprehension Questions

1. **What did Kate do at the beginning of the story?**
    (She rode up the elevator of the Empire State Building.)

2. **What was special about the Empire State Building?**
    (It was once the tallest building in New York City—and the world.)

3. **How did Kate plan to share her experience?**
    (She took pictures to share with her classmates.)

Passage	Words: 151			
Oral Reading Accuracy				%
Reading Rate				wpm
Comprehension # Correct				/3
Fluency	1	2	3	4

Name _____ Date _____

Alexander Graham Bell

1   Alexander Graham Bell worked for many years with people who could not hear. He was a speech teacher and opened a special school in Boston.

2   In 1874, he had an idea for an invention. He wanted to develop something called the speaking telegraph. He planned to send the sound of a human voice over a wire using electricity.

3   On March 10, 1876, Bell succeeded. He was upstairs working in his lab while his assistant, Thomas Watson, was in the basement. Bell spoke into the mouthpiece of his invention. He said, "Mr. Watson, come here. I want you."

4   Watson heard these words. Watson ran up three flights of stairs, calling, "I can hear you! I can hear you!"

5   Alexander Graham Bell had invented the telephone!

6   Bell's invention made him a lot of money. For the rest of his life, he used his wealth and knowledge to help people who were deaf.

Name _____ Date _____

Alexander Graham Bell

Words per Line

1   Alexander Graham Bell worked for many years with people who could not hear. He was a speech teacher and opened a special school in Boston.

_____8
_____19
_____25

2   In 1874, he had an idea for an invention. He wanted to develop something called the speaking telegraph. He planned to send the sound of a human voice over a wire using electricity.

_____36
_____44
_____56
_____58

3   On March 10, 1876, Bell succeeded. He was upstairs working in his lab while his assistant, Thomas Watson, was in the basement. Bell spoke into the mouthpiece of his invention. He said, "Mr. Watson, come here. I want you."

_____67
_____76
_____86
_____96
97

4   Watson heard these words. Watson ran up three flights of stairs, calling, "I can hear you! I can hear you!"

_____106
_____117

5   Alexander Graham Bell had invented the telephone!

_____124

6   Bell's invention made him a lot of money. For the rest of his life, he used his wealth and knowledge to help people who were deaf.

_____135
_____146
_____150

Comprehension Questions

1.   **What is this passage mostly about?**

    (Alexander Graham Bell and his invention of the telephone)

2.   **How did Bell discover that his invention worked?**

    (He spoke into it, and his assistant three floors below heard his voice.)

3.   **Besides inventing things, what else did Bell do?**

    (He was a speech teacher and helped people who could not hear.)

Passage	Words: 150			
Oral Reading Accuracy				%
Reading Rate				wpm
Comprehension # Correct				/3
Fluency	1	2	3	4

Name _____ Date _____

A Bundle of Sticks

1   The village carpenter had a fine shop and three strong sons. But sometimes it took all night to finish an order. Instead of working together, the boys argued all the time and accomplished very little.

2   Now the carpenter had to go away on a business trip. How could his sons manage the shop when they never agreed on anything?

3   To teach his sons a lesson, the carpenter gathered them in the workshop. He gave each son a stick and told him to break it. *Snap*, *snap*, *snap*, went the sticks, and the boys argued over who broke his stick first.

4   Then the carpenter gave each boy a bundle of sticks. Despite their best efforts, the sons could not break them.

5   The carpenter noted that each stick alone snapped easily. But bundled together, the sticks were unbreakable.

6   "Alone," he said, "you are weaker. But united, you have great strength."

Grades K–6 • Benchmark Advance • **Fluency** Quick Checks • © Benchmark Education Company, LLC

Name _____ Date _____

A Bundle of Sticks

Words per Line

1   The village carpenter had a fine shop and three strong   ____10
sons. But sometimes it took all night to finish an order.   ____21
Instead of working together, the boys argued all the time   ____31
and accomplished very little.   ____35

2   Now the carpenter had to go away on a business trip.   ____46
How could his sons manage the shop when they never   ____56
agreed on anything?   ____59

3   To teach his sons a lesson, the carpenter gathered   ____68
them in the workshop. He gave each son a stick and told   ____80
him to break it. *Snap*, *snap*, *snap*, went the sticks, and   ____91
the boys argued over who broke his stick first.   ____100

4   Then the carpenter gave each boy a bundle of sticks.   ____110
Despite their best efforts, the sons could not break them.   ____120

5   The carpenter noted that each stick alone snapped   ____128
easily. But bundled together, the sticks were unbreakable.   ____136

6   "Alone," he said, "you are weaker. But united, you have   ____146
great strength."   ____148

Comprehension Questions

1.   **What was the carpenter's problem?**
     (His sons argued all the time and did not get their work done.)

2.   **Why did the boys have to manage the shop by themselves?**
     (The father was going away on a business trip.)

3.   **What is the lesson in this story?**
     (There is strength in unity, OR we are stronger when we work together.)

Passage	Words: 148			
Oral Reading Accuracy				%
Reading Rate				wpm
Comprehension # Correct				/3
Fluency	1	2	3	4

Name _____ Date _____

The Liberty Bell

1   Every year, millions of people visit the Liberty Bell in Philadelphia, Pennsylvania. At one time, Philadelphia was the nation's capital.

2   Today, the Liberty Bell represents freedom. But when it was first used in 1751, it called lawmakers to attend their meetings. It also alerted townspeople to gather in the town square to hear the reading of the news. At the time, it was called the State House Bell.

3   On July 8, 1776, the Liberty Bell rang. It called people to the center of town to hear the first public reading of the Declaration of Independence. This document declared the thirteen American colonies free from British rule. A new nation was born.

4   People who were against slavery adopted the bell as a symbol of freedom for their movement. They named it "The Liberty Bell" in the 1830s. The bell then became a great symbol of freedom nationwide.

Name _____ Date _____

The Liberty Bell

Words per Line

1   Every year, millions of people visit the Liberty Bell in Philadelphia, Pennsylvania. At one time, Philadelphia was the nation's capital.

_____10
_____17
_____20

2   Today, the Liberty Bell represents freedom. But when it was first used in 1751, it called lawmakers to attend their meetings. It also alerted townspeople to gather in the town square to hear the reading of the news. At the time, it was called the State House Bell.

_____28
_____39
_____48
_____60
_____68

3   On July 8, 1776, the Liberty Bell rang. It called people to the center of town to hear the first public reading of the Declaration of Independence. This document declared the thirteen American colonies free from British rule. A new nation was born.

_____79
_____91
_____98
_____107
_____111

4   People who were against slavery adopted the bell as a symbol of freedom for their movement. They named it "The Liberty Bell" in the 1830s. The bell then became a great symbol of freedom nationwide.

_____121
_____130
_____141
_____146

Comprehension Questions

1. **What was the Liberty Bell first used for?**
    (It called lawmakers to meetings and called townspeople to the town square to hear the news.)

2. **Why did the Liberty Bell ring in Philadelphia on July 8, 1776?**
    (It called people to hear the first public reading of the Declaration of Independence OR The colonies had declared their independence from Britain.)

3. **Who named the bell "The Liberty Bell"?**
    (people who were against slavery)

Passage	Words: 146			
Oral Reading Accuracy				%
Reading Rate				wpm
Comprehension # Correct				/3
Fluency	1	2	3	4

Name _____ Date _____

Camels

1   Camels are large animals that have either one or two humps on their backs. The kind that have one hump are known as dromedary camels and live mainly in the desert. People have been riding these camels and using them to carry goods for more than 3,000 years. Some people call them the "ships of the desert."

2   Camels can carry large loads for long distances. Carrying two hundred pounds while walking twenty miles in the blazing sun is an easy feat for a camel. Camels can also go a long time without food or water. The humps on their backs store fat for this very reason.

3   These animals are well suited for desert life. Camels have a thin piece of skin over each eye. They also have a double row of eyelashes. These protect the camels from desert sandstorms. Camels can close their nostrils, too. This protects their noses from windblown sand.

Name _____ Date _____

Camels

Words per Line

1   Camels are large animals that have either one or two   ____10
humps on their backs. The kind that have one hump   ____20
are known as dromedary camels and live mainly in the   ____30
desert. People have been riding these camels and using   ____39
them to carry goods for more than 3,000 years. Some   ____49
people call them the "ships of the desert."   ____57

2   Camels can carry large loads for long distances.   ____65
Carrying two hundred pounds while walking twenty miles   ____73
in the blazing sun is an easy feat for a camel. Camels can   ____86
also go a long time without food or water. The humps on   ____98
their backs store fat for this very reason.   ____106

3   These animals are well suited for desert life. Camels   ____115
have a thin piece of skin over each eye. They also have   ____127
a double row of eyelashes. These protect the camels from   ____137
desert sandstorms. Camels can close their nostrils, too.   ____145
This protects their noses from windblown sand.   ____152

Comprehension Questions

1. **Why do some people call camels the "ships of the desert"?**
   (Camels carry goods and people, as ships do.)

2. **Why do camels have humps?**
   (They store fat in their humps so they can go a long time without food or water.)

3. **Explain two ways camels' eyes are well suited for desert life.**
   (They have skin over their eyes and a double row of eyelashes to keep sand out.)

Passage	Words: 152			
Oral Reading Accuracy				%
Reading Rate				wpm
Comprehension # Correct				/3
Fluency	1	2	3	4

Name _____ Date _____

A Fine Gift

1   Some time ago, a young man named Omar lived in a small village. Omar longed for respect, so one day he went to see the local blacksmith.

2   "People admire a great hunter," Omar told him, "so make me a fine sword."

3   When Omar returned days later for his weapon, the blacksmith gave him a beautiful wooden platter.

4   "Are you a woodcarver or a blacksmith?" Omar cried. "I asked for a sword."

5   The blacksmith explained that to gain respect, Omar should fill the platter with food for the villagers. Omar was angry, but he decided to try the blacksmith's idea. He piled the platter with food and held a feast. After word spread about Omar's generosity, he held feasts every month. They brought people together and spread good will.

6   After Omar became village chief, he gave the blacksmith a healthy large cow. Both men agreed they had received a fine gift.

Grades K–6 • Benchmark Advance • **Fluency** Quick Checks • © Benchmark Education Company, LLC

Name _____ Date _____

A Fine Gift

Words per Line

1   Some time ago, a young man named Omar lived in
a small village. Omar longed for respect, so one day
he went to see the local blacksmith.

_____10
_____20
_____27

2   "People admire a great hunter," Omar told him,
"so make me a fine sword."

_____35
_____41

3   When Omar returned days later for his weapon, the
blacksmith gave him a beautiful wooden platter.

_____50
_____57

4   "Are you a woodcarver or a blacksmith?" Omar cried.
"I asked for a sword."

_____66
_____71

5   The blacksmith explained that to gain respect, Omar
should fill the platter with food for the villagers. Omar
was angry, but he decided to try the blacksmith's idea.
He piled the platter with food and held a feast. After
word spread about Omar's generosity, he held feasts
every month. They brought people together and spread
good will.

_____79
_____89
_____99
_____110
_____118
_____126
_____128

6   After Omar became village chief, he gave the
blacksmith a healthy large cow. Both men agreed they
had received a fine gift.

_____136
_____145
_____150

Comprehension Questions

1.   **Why did Omar want a sword?**
(He wanted people to respect him.)

2.   **What did the blacksmith give Omar, and why?**
(a wooden platter, to help Omar gain the people's respect)

3.   **Why did Omar give the blacksmith a cow?**
(to repay him for his good advice, OR as a gift)

Passage	Words: 150			
Oral Reading Accuracy				%
Reading Rate				wpm
Comprehension # Correct				/3
Fluency	1	2	3	4

Name _____ Date _____

Animal Habitats

1   An animal's habitat is where it lives. A habitat provides an animal with what it needs to survive: food, water, and shelter.

2   Some animal habitats are in trouble, mainly because people have moved in. Factories, cars, and farms pollute the water and air. People drain water from lakes and rivers to build new houses and shopping malls. In addition, they cut down trees and pave over grassy areas where animals live.

3   Some animals are able to adapt to living with people. For example, the peregrine falcon usually lives high up on a cliff. But in some cities, falcons now build their nests on the tops of buildings instead. Small animals such as foxes usually live in forests and meadows. Now, in some places, you may see them living on a golf course or in a housing development instead.

4   Many people want to protect the places where animals live. They want to conserve the land so animals can live in their natural habitats.

Name _____ Date _____

Animal Habitats

Words per Line

1   An animal's habitat is where it lives. A habitat provides   ____10
an animal with what it needs to survive: food, water, and   ____21
shelter.   ____22

2   Some animal habitats are in trouble, mainly because   ____30
people have moved in. Factories, cars, and farms pollute   ____39
the water and air. People drain water from lakes and   ____49
rivers to build new houses and shopping malls. In   ____58
addition, they cut down trees and pave over grassy areas   ____68
where animals live.   ____71

3   Some animals are able to adapt to living with people.   ____81
For example, the peregrine falcon usually lives high up on   ____91
a cliff. But in some cities, falcons now build their nests   ____102
on the tops of buildings instead. Small animals such as   ____112
foxes usually live in forests and meadows. Now, in some   ____122
places, you may see them living on a golf course or in a   ____135
housing development instead.   ____138

4   Many people want to protect the places where animals   ____147
live. They want to conserve the land so animals can live   ____158
in their natural habitats.   ____162

Comprehension Questions

1.   **What is this passage mostly about?**
(animal habitats)

2.   **In what ways do people affect animal habitats?**
(People cause pollution and destroy habitats by building houses and shopping malls.)

3.   **How has the peregrine falcon adapted to losing its habitat?**
(It now builds its nest on tops of buildings instead of on cliffs.)

Passage	Words: 162			
Oral Reading Accuracy				%
Reading Rate				wpm
Comprehension # Correct				/3
Fluency	1	2	3	4

Name _____ Date _____

Climates in the United States

1   People like to talk about the weather and how it changes every day. Climate is different from weather. Climate is the average pattern of weather in a certain region. It is measured over many years.

2   There are seven different climate regions in the United States. One region is the Northwest, which includes states such as Oregon and Washington. This region has cool and wet winters near the Pacific coast. Inland areas are cool and dry. Heavy snow falls during the winter in the mountains. In the summer, the temperature stays cooler than in other parts of the country, especially along the coast.

3   On the other side of the country is the Southeast region, which includes Florida, Georgia, and other states. Its climate is mostly warm and sunny. Temperatures are usually mild in the winter. It is hot and humid during the summer.

Name _____ Date _____

Climates in the United States

Words per Line

1   People like to talk about the weather and how it changes every day. Climate is different from weather. Climate is the average pattern of weather in a certain region. It is measured over many years.

____10
____18
____28
____35

2   There are seven different climate regions in the United States. One region is the Northwest, which includes states such as Oregon and Washington. This region has cool and wet winters near the Pacific coast. Inland areas are cool and dry. Heavy snow falls during the winter in the mountains. In the summer, the temperature stays cooler than in other parts of the country, especially along the coast.

____43
____51
____59
____69
____79
____88
____97
____102

3   On the other side of the country is the Southeast region, which includes Florida, Georgia, and other states. Its climate is mostly warm and sunny. Temperatures are usually mild in the winter. It is hot and humid during the summer.

____112
____120
____129
____140
____142

 Comprehension Questions

1. **How is climate different from weather?**
    (Weather changes every day, but climate is the normal weather pattern over a long period of time.)

2. **What is the climate like in the Southeast region?**
    (It is usually warm and sunny.)

3. **How are winters different in the Northwest and the Southeast?**
    (They are cool, wet, and snowy in the Northwest, but mild in the Southeast.)

Passage	Words: 142			
Oral Reading Accuracy				%
Reading Rate				wpm
Comprehension # Correct				/3
Fluency	1	2	3	4

Name _____ Date _____

The Beach

1   The Velez family packed for their vacation by the ocean. Mom, Dad, Tim, and Eve planned to spend the week in a small house near the beach. It took the family all day to drive there.

2   The next morning, Tim and Eve rode their bikes on a path by the ocean. After lunch, they went swimming and diving in the waves. Then they made sand castles near the water.

3   As the sun set, the family watched the waves come in. "The beach is so peaceful now," said Mom.

4   When Tim and Eve went back to the beach the next morning, their sand castles were gone. "The tide came in and washed your sand castles away," explained Mom.

5   "Look!" shouted Eve. "The ocean took our sand castles, but the ocean left us a surprise."

6   Tim and Eve saw beautiful shells all over the beach. "I know what we can do today," said Tim.

Name _____ Date _____

The Beach

Words per Line

1   The Velez family packed for their vacation by the   ___9
ocean. Mom, Dad, Tim, and Eve planned to spend the   ___19
week in a small house near the beach. It took the   ___30
family all day to drive there.   ___36

2   The next morning, Tim and Eve rode their bikes on   ___46
a path by the ocean. After lunch, they went swimming   ___56
and diving in the waves. Then they made sand castles   ___66
near the water.   ___69

3   As the sun set, the family watched the waves come   ___79
in. "The beach is so peaceful now," said Mom.   ___88

4   When Tim and Eve went back to the beach the next   ___99
morning, their sand castles were gone. "The tide came   ___108
in and washed your sand castles away," explained Mom.   ___117

5   "Look!" shouted Eve. "The ocean took our sand   ___125
castles, but the ocean left us a surprise."   ___133

6   Tim and Eve saw beautiful shells all over the beach.   ___143
"I know what we can do today," said Tim.   ___152

Comprehension Questions

1. **What is this passage mostly about?**
    (The Velez family goes on vacation at the beach.)

2. **What did Tim and Eve discover at the beach the second morning?**
    (Their sand castles were gone, but the beach was covered with shells.)

3. **What will Tim and Eve probably do next?**
    (They will probably collect seashells.)

Passage	Words: 152			
Oral Reading Accuracy				%
Reading Rate				wpm
Comprehension # Correct				/3
Fluency	1	2	3	4

Name _____ Date _____

Water

1   All living things need water to survive. Pure water has no color, odor, or taste, but it has three different states, or forms.

2   The most familiar form of water is liquid. We drink liquid water and use it to clean and cook. Rain, rivers, streams, and oceans are all liquids.

3   Water can also be a solid. When the air temperature gets cold enough, water freezes and turns to ice. Ice is lighter than liquid water. This is why ice cubes float. Icicles and snow are both solid forms of water.

4   Water can also be an odorless gas called water vapor. Water vapor is usually invisible, but it is in the air all around us. You can easily create water vapor by boiling water. Water vapor rises from the pot. Sometimes water vapor becomes visible as steam or fog.

Name _____ Date _____

Water

Words per Line

1   All living things need water to survive. Pure water
has no color, odor, or taste, but it has three different
states, or forms.

____9
____20
____23

2   The most familiar form of water is liquid. We drink
liquid water and use it to clean and cook. Rain, rivers,
streams, and oceans are all liquids.

____33
____44
____50

3   Water can also be a solid. When the air temperature
gets cold enough, water freezes and turns to ice. Ice
is lighter than liquid water. This is why ice cubes float.
Icicles and snow are both solid forms of water.

____60
____70
____81
____90

4   Water can also be an odorless gas called water vapor.
Water vapor is usually invisible, but it is in the air all
around us. You can easily create water vapor by boiling
water. Water vapor rises from the pot. Sometimes water
vapor becomes visible as steam or fog.

____100
____112
____122
____131
____138

 Comprehension Questions

1. **What is the main idea of this passage?**
    (There are three forms of water—liquid, solid, and gas.)

2. **Why do ice cubes float?**
    (Ice is lighter than liquid water.)

3. **How can you create water vapor?**
    (by boiling water)

Passage	Words: 138			
Oral Reading Accuracy				**%**
Reading Rate				**wpm**
Comprehension # Correct				**/3**
Fluency	1	2	3	4

Name _____ Date _____

Where Stars Are Born

1   All stars are born in the same way. They begin in
a nebula (NEH-byuh-luh). This is a thick cloud of gas
and dust in space.

2   There are different types of nebulas. Some nebulas
give off light, and some reflect the light of stars
around them. A dark nebula comprises so much dust
and gas that it blocks out all light around it. But
astronomers believe this is where stars are born.

3   Inside the dark nebula, gas and dust stick together
and form clumps. A large clump has more gravity.
This gravity can pull other particles of gas and dust to
the clump. With more particles, the clump increases in
mass.

4   The thickly packed gas and dust create a very hot,
dense space in the center of the clump. Eventually,
this core will vaporize the dust. Then the nebula
collapses. The collapse of a nebula is the beginning
of a star's birth.

Name _____ Date _____

Where Stars Are Born

Words per Line

1   All stars are born in the same way. They begin in   ___11
a nebula (NEH-byuh-luh). This is a thick cloud of gas   ___20
and dust in space.   ___24

2   There are different types of nebulas. Some nebulas   ___32
give off light, and some reflect the light of stars   ___42
around them. A dark nebula comprises so much dust   ___51
and gas that it blocks out all light around it. But   ___62
astronomers believe this is where stars are born.   ___70

3   Inside the dark nebula, gas and dust stick together   ___79
and form clumps. A large clump has more gravity.   ___88
This gravity can pull other particles of gas and dust to   ___99
the clump. With more particles, the clump increases in   ___108
mass.   ___109

4   The thickly packed gas and dust create a very hot,   ___119
dense space in the center of the clump. Eventually,   ___128
this core will vaporize the dust. Then the nebula   ___137
collapses. The collapse of a nebula is the beginning   ___146
of a star's birth.   ___150

Comprehension Questions

1.   **What is this passage mostly about?**
      (how stars form)

2.   **What is a nebula?**
      (a thick cloud of gas and dust in space)

3.   **What happens when a nebula collapses?**
      (A star forms.)

Passage	Words: 150			
Oral Reading Accuracy				%
Reading Rate				wpm
Comprehension # Correct				/3
Fluency	1	2	3	4

Name _____ Date _____

The Youngest Senator

1   Max Kidd walked up the steps of the Capitol Building in Washington, D.C. He was the first ten-year-old elected to Congress, and today was his first day on the job. News reporters wanted to hear about the senator's plans.

2   "I plan to introduce a bill to stop air and water pollution," Max explained. "We need to do a better job of protecting our planet."

3   "I want to support the arts, music, and physical education in school. In some schools, these classes are being cut short in favor of reading and math," Max explained. "Of course, reading and math are very important, but let's not forget the arts."

4   "Senator, it sounds like you are well prepared for the job," said one reporter.

5   Suddenly, Max woke up to the sound of his alarm clock. He rubbed his eyes and glanced at his nightstand. "What a strange dream," he said to himself.

Name _____ Date _____

The Youngest Senator

Words per Line

1   Max Kidd walked up the steps of the Capitol Building   ___10
in Washington, D.C. He was the first ten-year-old   ___19
elected to Congress, and today was his first day on   ___29
the job. News reporters wanted to hear about the   ___38
senator's plans.   ___40

2   "I plan to introduce a bill to stop air and water   ___51
pollution," Max explained. "We need to do a better job   ___61
of protecting our planet."   ___65

3   "I want to support the arts, music, and physical   ___74
education in school. In some schools, these classes   ___82
are being cut short in favor of reading and math,"   ___92
Max explained. "Of course, reading and math are very   ___101
important, but let's not forget the arts."   ___108

4   "Senator, it sounds like you are well prepared for   ___117
the job," said one reporter.   ___122

5   Suddenly, Max woke up to the sound of his   ___131
alarm clock. He rubbed his eyes and glanced at   ___140
his nightstand. "What a strange dream," he said to   ___149
himself.   ___150

Comprehension Questions

1. **Why do the reporters want to talk to Max?**
    (He is the youngest senator in history.)

2. **What two issues are important to Max?**
    (Stopping pollution and supporting art, music, and physical education in schools.)

3. **What happens at the end of the story?**
    (Max wakes up from his dream.)

Passage	Words: 150			
Oral Reading Accuracy				%
Reading Rate				wpm
Comprehension # Correct				/3
Fluency	1	2	3	4

Name _____ Date _____

The Rainbow Mailbox

1   Lana and her mom wanted to make a new mailbox for their house. The old one had started to rust.

2   "How about a dinosaur mailbox?" Mom suggested. "You love dinosaurs."

3   "That's not very colorful," said Lana. "I think having something colorful will make the front of our house cheery, especially in the winter when it's gloomy and snowy. Why don't we build a rainbow mailbox with many colors?"

4   After Lana and her mom went to the paint store, Lana spent two hours carefully painting a rainbow on a new mailbox. Then she set the mailbox on the back porch to dry.

5   The next day, Lana and her mom set up the mailbox at the end of their driveway. They finished just as the mail carrier arrived.

6   When the mail carrier saw the new mailbox, he said, "Wow, this is the most colorful mailbox on the block!"

Name _____ Date _____

The Rainbow Mailbox

Words per Line

1   Lana and her mom wanted to make a new mailbox
for their house. The old one had started to rust.

____10
____20

2   "How about a dinosaur mailbox?" Mom suggested.
"You love dinosaurs."

____27
____30

3   "That's not very colorful," said Lana. "I think having
something colorful will make the front of our house
cheery, especially in the winter when it's gloomy and
snowy. Why don't we build a rainbow mailbox with
many colors?"

____39
____48
____57
____66
____68

4   After Lana and her mom went to the paint store,
Lana spent two hours carefully painting a rainbow on
a new mailbox. Then she set the mailbox on the back
porch to dry.

____78
____87
____98
____101

5   The next day, Lana and her mom set up the mailbox
at the end of their driveway. They finished just as the
mail carrier arrived.

____112
____123
____126

6   When the mail carrier saw the new mailbox, he said,
"Wow, this is the most colorful mailbox on the block!"

____136
____146

Comprehension Questions

1. **Why does Lana decide against making a dinosaur mailbox?**
(It is not very colorful.)

2. **Where do Lana and her mom go?**
(to the paint store)

3. **What happens at the end of the story?**
(Lana and her mom set up the new mailbox, and the mail carrier compliments them.)

Passage	Words: 146			
Oral Reading Accuracy				%
Reading Rate				wpm
Comprehension # Correct				/3
Fluency	1	2	3	4

Name _____ Date _____

The Rescue

1   The Bartons were hiking near their cabin when they came to a river. There had been a lot of rain in recent days. As a result, the river was flowing very fast. "We'll have to wait for the river to go down before we cross," warned Mom.

2   "Look, the river's rising, and the water is getting near our cabin," Jordan alerted his parents.

3   As the water continued to rise, Dad and Mom became worried. They told Jordan to pack up and prepare to leave.

4   "We should get to higher ground before the river crests," said Dad.

5   But it was too late. The river had already begun flowing over its banks. Luckily, the Bartons had a canoe at their cabin. They quickly got in, put on their life vests, and felt the water lift the canoe up. Dad used a rope to tie the canoe to a tree, and they waited there until the park ranger pulled up in a rescue boat to help them.

Name _____ Date _____

The Rescue

Words per Line

1   The Bartons were hiking near their cabin when they
came to a river. There had been a lot of rain in recent
days. As a result, the river was flowing very fast. "We'll
have to wait for the river to go down before we cross,"
warned Mom.

____9
____22
____33
____45
____47

2   "Look, the river's rising, and the water is getting near
our cabin," Jordan alerted his parents.

____57
____63

3   As the water continued to rise, Dad and Mom became
worried. They told Jordan to pack up and prepare to
leave.

____73
____83
____84

4   "We should get to higher ground before the river
crests," said Dad.

____93
____96

5   But it was too late. The river had already begun
flowing over its banks. Luckily, the Bartons had a canoe
at their cabin. They quickly got in, put on their life
vests, and felt the water lift the canoe up. Dad used a
rope to tie the canoe to a tree, and they waited there
until the park ranger pulled up in a rescue boat to help
them.

____106
____116
____127
____139
____151
____163
____164

Comprehension Questions

1.   **What happened to the Bartons?**
(They got caught in a flood.)

2.   **Why were Mom and Dad worried?**
(The river was rising fast.)

3.   **How did the family stay safe?**
(They got into their canoe, tied it to a tree, and waited to be rescued.)

Passage	Words: 164			
Oral Reading Accuracy				%
Reading Rate				wpm
Comprehension # Correct				/3
Fluency	1	2	3	4

Name _____ Date _____

Volcanoes

1   A volcano is an opening where molten rock from inside Earth makes its way to the surface. What causes a volcanic eruption? Volcanoes erupt when pressure within Earth forces magma to the surface. Magma is molten rock. It collects deep underground in a magma chamber. As the magma collects, it produces hot gases. The pressure of the gas in the magma forces the magma upward. The magma rises and bursts through the crust in weak spots called vents. When it reaches Earth's surface, it is called lava.

2   All volcanoes release gases during an eruption. Most volcanoes erupt with lava. Some erupt with rocks, too. If the magma contains a lot of gas, it will burst out with rock fragments. The pressure of the gas sends chunks of rock blasting out of the volcano. Some volcanoes alternate between eruptions of lava and eruptions of rocks. When a volcano erupts, it can spew out anything from fine particles of dust to huge blocks of rock as big as a house.

Name _____ Date _____

Volcanoes

Words per Line

1   A volcano is an opening where molten rock from
inside Earth makes its way to the surface. What
causes a volcanic eruption? Volcanoes erupt when
pressure within Earth forces magma to the surface.
Magma is molten rock. It collects deep underground in
a magma chamber. As the magma collects, it produces
hot gases. The pressure of the gas in the magma
forces the magma upward. The magma rises and bursts
through the crust in weak spots called vents. When it
reaches Earth's surface, it is called lava.

____9
____18
____25
____33
____42
____51
____61
____70
____80
____87

2   All volcanoes release gases during an eruption. Most
volcanoes erupt with lava. Some erupt with rocks, too.
If the magma contains a lot of gas, it will burst out
with rock fragments. The pressure of the gas sends
chunks of rock blasting out of the volcano. Some
volcanoes alternate between eruptions of lava and
eruptions of rocks. When a volcano erupts, it can spew
out anything from fine particles of dust to huge blocks
of rock as big as a house.

____95
____104
____116
____125
____134
____141
____151
____161
____168

Comprehension Questions

1. **What causes a volcano to erupt?**
    (Pressure inside Earth builds up and forces magma to the surface.)

2. **What comes out of a volcano when it erupts?**
    (gases, lava, rocks)

3. **What is the difference between magma and lava?**
    (Molten rock inside Earth is magma. When it reaches the surface, magma becomes lava.)

Passage	Words: 168			
Oral Reading Accuracy				%
Reading Rate				wpm
Comprehension # Correct				/3
Fluency	1	2	3	4

Name _____ Date _____

Howler Monkeys

1   Have you ever heard a howler monkey cry out? If
you have, you understand how the howler monkey
got its name! When many howler monkeys get together,
their cries can be heard up to three miles away!

2   Howler monkeys use their strong, loud voices as
a signal to other monkeys. Their cries mean: "Stay
away! This territory belongs to our troop." Up to fifteen
monkeys live in a troop. Howler monkeys rarely have
to fight to defend their territory. Their cries are warning
enough to keep other monkeys away.

3   Male howler monkeys have large throats and huge
vocal cords. This allows them to raise the volume of
their cries. Even though they are loud, they do not have
a piercing screech. Their cries sound more like deep
bellows or groans.

4   Howler monkeys live in the tropical rain forests of
Central and South America.

Grades K–6 • Benchmark Advance • **Fluency** Quick Checks • © Benchmark Education Company, LLC

Name _____ Date _____

Howler Monkeys

Words per Line

1   Have you ever heard a howler monkey cry out? If   ____10
you have, you understand how the howler monkey   ____18
got its name! When many howler monkeys get together,   ____27
their cries can be heard up to three miles away!   ____37

2   Howler monkeys use their strong, loud voices as   ____45
a signal to other monkeys. Their cries mean: "Stay   ____54
away! This territory belongs to our troop." Up to fifteen   ____64
monkeys live in a troop. Howler monkeys rarely have   ____73
to fight to defend their territory. Their cries are warning   ____83
enough to keep other monkeys away.   ____89

3   Male howler monkeys have large throats and huge   ____97
vocal cords. This allows them to raise the volume of   ____107
their cries. Even though they are loud, they do not have   ____118
a piercing screech. Their cries sound more like deep   ____127
bellows or groans.   ____130

4   Howler monkeys live in the tropical rain forests of   ____139
Central and South America.   ____143

Comprehension Questions

1.   **How did the howler monkey get its name?**
      (It makes really loud sounds.)

2.   **Why do howler monkeys cry out?**
      (to claim their territory, OR to warn other monkeys to keep away)

3.   **In what kind of place do howler monkeys live?**
      (tropical rain forest)

Passage	Words: 143			
Oral Reading Accuracy				%
Reading Rate				wpm
Comprehension # Correct				/3
Fluency	1	2	3	4

Name _____ Date _____

The Nobel Prize

1   The Nobel Prize is a highly valued award given for outstanding achievement in science, medicine, economics, literature, or the promotion of peace. The first prizes were awarded in 1901. Prizes are generally awarded to individuals. However, small groups of people and organizations have also won at different times.

2   Inventor Alfred Nobel established the prize. Nobel was from Sweden. His inventions, discoveries, and books earned him a great amount of wealth. In his will, he explained that he wanted his fortune to be used to fund these awards. He requested that one be a peace prize.

3   The first Nobel Peace Prize was given to Frédéric Passy of France and Henry Dunant of Switzerland. Passy brought together an international peace movement. Dunant was the founder of the Red Cross, an organization that helps people in need. Notable Americans who have won the prize include Martin Luther King Jr., Theodore Roosevelt, and Barack Obama.

Name _____ Date _____

The Nobel Prize

Words per Line

1 The Nobel Prize is a highly valued award given   ___9
for outstanding achievement in science, medicine,   ___15
economics, literature, or the promotion of peace. The   ___23
first prizes were awarded in 1901. Prizes are generally   ___32
awarded to individuals. However, small groups of people   ___40
and organizations have also won at different times.   ___48

2 Inventor Alfred Nobel established the prize. Nobel was   ___56
from Sweden. His inventions, discoveries, and books   ___63
earned him a great amount of wealth. In his will, he   ___74
explained that he wanted his fortune to be used to   ___84
fund these awards. He requested that one be a peace   ___94
prize.   ___95

3 The first Nobel Peace Prize was given to Frédéric   ___104
Passy of France and Henry Dunant of Switzerland.   ___112
Passy brought together an international peace   ___118
movement. Dunant was the founder of the Red Cross,   ___127
an organization that helps people in need. Notable   ___135
Americans who have won the prize include Martin   ___143
Luther King Jr., Theodore Roosevelt, and Barack Obama.   ___151

Comprehension Questions

1. **How does someone win a Nobel Prize?**
    (by doing good work in science, medicine, economics, literature, or the promotion of peace)

2. **What kind of person was Alfred Nobel? Tell why you think so.**
    (He was very generous. He wanted his money to go to something good.)

3. **What was the first Nobel Peace Prize awarded for?**
    (It recognized the organizer of a peace movement and the founder of the Red Cross.)

Passage	Words: 151			
Oral Reading Accuracy				%
Reading Rate				wpm
Comprehension # Correct				/3
Fluency	1	2	3	4

Name _____ Date _____

A Big Scoop

1   Benson was a nosy guy who was always looking for interesting stories to write in the school newspaper.

2   "What are you doing, Martha?" asked Benson, looking over Martha's shoulder.

3   Martha was sitting by the garden pond.

4   "Go away, Benson, because this is a top secret operation and I don't want you or anyone else to know about it," said Martha.

5   "Oh, have you found something interesting for me to report in the school newspaper?" inquired Benson.

6   Martha thought for a minute before she smiled and said, "Don't tell, but there's a talking dogfish from Planet Dingo in the pond. It was delivered in this spaceship."

7   Just then Martha pulled out a shiny silver machine used to clean the pond.

8   The following day, Benson's newspaper report made the front page: "Talking Dogfish from Planet Dingo Lands in Local Pond!"

9   Benson had forgotten that it was April Fools' Day, and the joke was on him!

Name _____ Date _____

A Big Scoop

Words per Line

1   Benson was a nosy guy who was always looking for   ___10
    interesting stories to write in the school newspaper.   ___18

2   "What are you doing, Martha?" asked Benson, looking   ___26
    over Martha's shoulder.   ___29

3   Martha was sitting by the garden pond.   ___36

4   "Go away, Benson, because this is a top secret   ___45
    operation and I don't want you or anyone else to know   ___56
    about it," said Martha.   ___60

5   "Oh, have you found something interesting for me   ___68
    to report in the school newspaper?" inquired Benson.   ___76

6   Martha thought for a minute before she smiled   ___84
    and said, "Don't tell, but there's a talking dogfish   ___93
    from Planet Dingo in the pond. It was delivered in   ___103
    this spaceship."   ___105

7   Just then Martha pulled out a shiny silver machine   ___114
    used to clean the pond.   ___119

8   The following day, Benson's newspaper report made   ___126
    the front page: "Talking Dogfish from Planet Dingo   ___134
    Lands in Local Pond!"   ___138

9   Benson had forgotten that it was April Fools' Day,   ___147
    and the joke was on him!   ___153

Comprehension Questions

1. **What kind of person is Benson? Tell how you know.**
    (He is nosy, curious, and gullible. He believed Martha's report.)

2. **What did Martha tell Benson was in her pond?**
    (a talking dogfish from another planet)

3. **Why did Martha play a joke on Benson?** *(It was April Fools' Day.)*

Passage	Words: 153			
Oral Reading Accuracy				%
Reading Rate				wpm
Comprehension # Correct				/3
Fluency	1	2	3	4

Name _____   Date _____

Cutting Down on Trash

1   You eat a banana and throw away the peel, and then you empty your backpack and toss your old math papers. You pour a glass of milk and throw away the carton. Sadly, most of this normal, daily garbage ends up in a trash bin—and then in a landfill.

2   Some people have found a different way to handle trash: reuse items in a new way. They put things like grass clippings and eggshells in a pile outdoors to make compost, a rich soil for the garden. They use the backs of junk mail letters—in place of new paper—in their computer printer. They use an empty green bean can to hold markers on a desk. The list goes on and on.

3   So what about your trash? The banana peel can go in your new compost pile; the family can write grocery lists on the backs of your old math papers; you can make a bird feeder from the milk carton. Now you have reused instead of throwing away!

Name _____ Date _____

Cutting Down on Trash

Words per Line

1   You eat a banana and throw away the peel, and   ____10
then you empty your backpack and toss your old math   ____20
papers. You pour a glass of milk and throw away the   ____31
carton. Sadly, most of this normal, daily garbage ends   ____40
up in a trash bin—and then in a landfill.   ____50

2   Some people have found a different way to handle   ____59
trash: reuse items in a new way. They put things like   ____70
grass clippings and eggshells in a pile outdoors to make   ____80
compost, a rich soil for the garden. They use the backs   ____91
of junk mail letters—in place of new paper—in their   ____102
computer printer. They use an empty green bean can to   ____112
hold markers on a desk. The list goes on and on.   ____123

3   So what about your trash? The banana peel can go   ____133
in your new compost pile; the family can write grocery   ____143
lists on the backs of your old math papers; you can   ____154
make a bird feeder from the milk carton. Now you have   ____165
reused instead of throwing away!   ____170

Comprehension Questions

1. **According to this passage, where does most trash go?**
    (into a trash bin, then to a landfill)

2. **What does the author say to do with the old math papers?**
    (Write grocery lists on the back of them.)

3. **What is this passage mostly about?**
    (how to reuse your trash in new, useful ways)

Passage	Words: 170			
Oral Reading Accuracy				%
Reading Rate				wpm
Comprehension # Correct				/3
Fluency	1	2	3	4

Name _____ Date _____

The Cat Show

1   "I am going to enter Ebony in the big cat show, but first I have to give her a bath," said Jessie.

2   Ebony must have sensed that she was about to get a bath because she scrambled up a tall cottonwood tree. Jessie pleaded and pleaded for her to come down. But Ebony just sat high up in the tree, ignoring Jessie's pleas. Several neighbors came out and tried to help Jessie get Ebony down, but they had no success.

3   Jessie didn't know what to do, so she called the fire department. Soon firefighters were on the scene with their tall ladders. After much work, they got Ebony out of the tree and into Jessie's arms.

4   "Well, I guess I won't be entering you in the cat show," said Jessie. "But you sure put on a spectacular show for the neighbors."

Name _____ Date _____

The Cat Show

Words per Line

1   "I am going to enter Ebony in the big cat show, but
first I have to give her a bath," said Jessie.

___12
___22

2   Ebony must have sensed that she was about to get
a bath because she scrambled up a tall cottonwood
tree. Jessie pleaded and pleaded for her to come
down. But Ebony just sat high up in the tree, ignoring
Jessie's pleas. Several neighbors came out and tried to
help Jessie get Ebony down, but they had no success.

___32
___41
___50
___61
___70
___80

3   Jessie didn't know what to do, so she called the fire
department. Soon firefighters were on the scene with
their tall ladders. After much work, they got Ebony out
of the tree and into Jessie's arms.

___91
___99
___109
___116

4   "Well, I guess I won't be entering you in the cat
show," said Jessie. "But you sure put on a spectacular
show for the neighbors."

___127
___137
___141

Comprehension Questions

1.   **Why did the cat run up the tree?**
      (to avoid getting a bath)

2.   **How did Jessie get the cat down from the tree?**
      (She called the fire department for help.)

3.   **What was the "spectacular show" in the story?**
      (getting Ebony out of the tree)

Passage	Words: 141			
Oral Reading Accuracy				%
Reading Rate				wpm
Comprehension # Correct				/3
Fluency	1	2	3	4

Name _____ Date _____

Animal Adaptations

1   Many animals adapt to their surroundings by changing colors or behaviors. Camouflage is one way animals adapt. Animals use this technique to blend in with their surroundings. Blending in can protect them from predators or help them sneak up on their prey. Animals that use camouflage include the Arctic fox, the Arctic hare, and the ermine. These animals have brown fur in the summer and white fur in the winter.

2   Some animals adapt by changing their behavior. Monarch butterflies travel to certain areas of Mexico during the winter. Gray whales swim from the Arctic Ocean to the warmer Pacific to birth their calves.

3   Raccoons have changed their behavior in a different way. Long ago, when their habitats were less developed, raccoons nested in trees and ate things naturally found in the wild. But now humans have taken over much of their natural habitat. So raccoons have made themselves at home in people's attics, basements, and storage sheds. They forage through human garbage and eat what we have discarded.

Name _____ Date _____

Animal Adaptations

Words per Line

1   Many animals adapt to their surroundings by changing   ____8
colors or behaviors. Camouflage is one way animals   ____16
adapt. Animals use this technique to blend in with   ____25
their surroundings. Blending in can protect them from   ____33
predators or help them sneak up on their prey. Animals   ____43
that use camouflage include the Arctic fox, the Arctic   ____52
hare, and the ermine. These animals have brown fur in   ____62
the summer and white fur in the winter.   ____70

2   Some animals adapt by changing their behavior.   ____77
Monarch butterflies travel to certain areas of Mexico   ____85
during the winter. Gray whales swim from the Arctic   ____94
Ocean to the warmer Pacific to birth their calves.   ____103

3   Raccoons have changed their behavior in a different   ____111
way. Long ago, when their habitats were less developed,   ____120
raccoons nested in trees and ate things naturally found   ____129
in the wild. But now humans have taken over much of   ____140
their natural habitat. So raccoons have made themselves   ____148
at home in people's attics, basements, and storage   ____156
sheds. They forage through human garbage and eat   ____164
what we have discarded.   ____168

Comprehension Questions

1.   **Why does the author mention the Arctic fox, the Arctic hare, and the ermine?**
     (These animals change their appearances from summer to winter to blend in with their surroundings, OR they use camouflage.)

2.   **How do monarch butterflies change their behavior to adapt?**
     (They travel to Mexico during the winter.)

3.   **How have raccoons changed their behavior to adapt to their surroundings?**
     (They changed their habitat from trees to people's homes or sheds and now eat human garbage instead of things found in the wild.)

Passage	Words: 168			
Oral Reading Accuracy				%
Reading Rate				wpm
Comprehension # Correct				/3
Fluency	1	2	3	4

Name _____ Date _____

Fuzzy Faces Face Off

1   Every two years, more than 250 men compete in the World Beard and Moustache Championship. Contestants enter one or more of seventeen categories. Men are allowed to use wax and hair spray in some of the categories. However, they can't use hair color, hairpins, or hair extensions.

2   The purpose of the championship is to promote friendship between beard and moustache clubs throughout the world. The event also helps create standards in the growth and design of facial hair. Plus, club members have fun. They raise money for charity, march in parades, and make people smile.

3   One competitor's moustache stretches five feet from tip to tip before it is styled. He washes his moustache three times every morning. Another contestant has a beard styled to look like a snowshoe. He won the championship in 2009.

4   If you attend a competition, you might see a moustache twisted into the shape of a famous landmark or a beard that flows down to a man's shoes. As one winner said, "It feels fantastic to know I have the best beard in the world!"

Grades K–6 • Benchmark Advance • **Fluency** Quick Checks • © Benchmark Education Company, LLC

Name _____ Date _____

Fuzzy Faces Face Off

Words per Line

1 Every two years, more than 250 men compete in the	____10
World Beard and Moustache Championship. Contestants	____16
enter one or more of seventeen categories. Men are	____25
allowed to use wax and hair spray in some of the	____36
categories. However, they can't use hair color, hairpins,	____44
or hair extensions.	____47
2 The purpose of the championship is to promote	____55
friendship between beard and moustache clubs	____61
throughout the world. The event also helps create	____69
standards in the growth and design of facial hair. Plus,	____79
club members have fun. They raise money for charity,	____88
march in parades, and make people smile.	____95
3 One competitor's moustache stretches five feet from	____102
tip to tip before it is styled. He washes his moustache	____113
three times every morning. Another contestant has	____120
a beard styled to look like a snowshoe. He won the	____131
championship in 2009.	____134
4 If you attend a competition, you might see a	____143
moustache twisted into the shape of a famous landmark	____152
or a beard that flows down to a man's shoes. As one	____164
winner said, "It feels fantastic to know I have the best	____175
beard in the world!"	____179

Comprehension Questions

1. **What is the purpose of the World Beard and Moustache Championship?**
    (to promote friendship between beard and moustache clubs throughout the world)

2. **What items are not allowed as part of the World Beard and Moustache Championship?** *(Men cannot use hair color, hairpins, or hair extensions.)*

3. **Why would someone participate in the World Beard and Moustache Championship?**
    (to raise money, to win a prize, to show off his beard or moustache, to have fun)

Passage	Words: 179			
Oral Reading Accuracy				%
Reading Rate				wpm
Comprehension # Correct				/3
Fluency	1	2	3	4

Name _____ Date _____

Our Neighborhood in Space

1   Our solar system consists of all the planets that orbit around the sun. It also includes moons, comets, asteroids, and dwarf planets. The sun (which is actually a star) is at the center of the solar system, and all of the other objects travel around the sun.

2   Scientists are still trying to figure out how the solar system formed. Most believe dust and gas stuck together in clumps, and then stars ignited in the center of the clumps. The largest clump became the sun, and the smaller clumps became the planets and other objects. Since the solar system is billions of years old, it is difficult to know for sure how this happened.

3   There are eight major planets in the solar system. The inner planets—Mercury, Venus, Earth, and Mars—are mostly made of rock and metals. The outer planets are known as the gas giants. These planets—Jupiter, Saturn, Uranus, and Neptune—are mostly made of hydrogen and other gases. In between the two groups of planets lies the asteroid belt.

Name _____ Date _____

Our Neighborhood in Space

Words per Line

1   Our solar system consists of all the planets that
orbit around the sun. It also includes moons, comets,
asteroids, and dwarf planets. The sun (which is actually
a star) is at the center of the solar system, and all of
the other objects travel around the sun.

____9
____18
____27
____40
____47

2   Scientists are still trying to figure out how the
solar system formed. Most believe dust and gas stuck
together in clumps, and then stars ignited in the center
of the clumps. The largest clump became the sun,
and the smaller clumps became the planets and other
objects. Since the solar system is billions of years old,
it is difficult to know for sure how this happened.

____56
____65
____75
____84
____93
____103
____113

3   There are eight major planets in the solar system.
The inner planets—Mercury, Venus, Earth, and Mars—are
mostly made of rock and metals. The outer planets are
known as the gas giants. These planets—Jupiter, Saturn,
Uranus, and Neptune—are mostly made of hydrogen and
other gases. In between the two groups of planets lies
the asteroid belt.

____122
____131
____141
____150
____159
____169
____172

Comprehension Questions

1.   **What is this passage mostly about?**
      (the solar system)

2.   **How are the inner planets different from the outer planets?**
      *(The inner planets are made of rock and metals and are smaller, and the outer planets
      are gas giants.)*

3.   **How did the sun and planets form?**
      (Gas and dust stuck together in clumps. A star formed in the middle of the clumps.)

Passage	Words: 172			
Oral Reading Accuracy				%
Reading Rate				wpm
Comprehension # Correct				/3
Fluency	1	2	3	4

Name _____ Date _____

Scarecrow Joe

1   The old crows that circled around Farmer Randall's farm weren't afraid of Scarecrow Joe. Farmer Randall knew she had to do something because the crows were eating all of her corn and she needed her crop to earn money.

2   She decided to dress Joe in black clothes to make him look scarier. But the crows thought Joe looked like a big, black, friendly bird. They just kept eating Farmer Randall's corn and were not scared in the least.

3   Farmer Randall was stumped. She had to figure out a way to stop the crows, or her entire crop would be lost.

4   One day an eagle flew over the field and saw the crows eating Farmer Randall's corn. The eagle decided to help poor, frightened Scarecrow Joe by swooping down and scaring the crows. Alarmed, the crows flew away in a hurry and did not return. From that day on, the eagle and Scarecrow Joe kept Farmer Randall's corn safe.

Name _____ Date _____

Scarecrow Joe

Words per Line

1   The old crows that circled around Farmer Randall's farm   ___9
weren't afraid of Scarecrow Joe. Farmer Randall knew she   ___18
had to do something because the crows were eating all   ___28
of her corn and she needed her crop to earn money.   ___39

2   She decided to dress Joe in black clothes to make him   ___50
look scarier. But the crows thought Joe looked like a big,   ___61
black, friendly bird. They just kept eating Farmer Randall's   ___70
corn and were not scared in the least.   ___78

3   Farmer Randall was stumped. She had to figure out a   ___88
way to stop the crows, or her entire crop would be lost.   ___100

4   One day an eagle flew over the field and saw the   ___111
crows eating Farmer Randall's corn. The eagle decided to   ___120
help poor, frightened Scarecrow Joe by swooping down   ___128
and scaring the crows. Alarmed, the crows flew away in   ___138
a hurry and did not return. From that day on, the eagle   ___150
and Scarecrow Joe kept Farmer Randall's corn safe.   ___158

Comprehension Questions

1.   **What did Farmer Randall do to make Scarecrow Joe look scary?**
(dressed him in black clothes)

2.   **Why weren't the crows scared by Scarecrow Joe in his new outfit?**
(They thought he looked like a big, black, friendly bird.)

3.   **How did Farmer Randall's problem get solved?**
(An eagle came and scared the crows away.)

Passage	Words: 158			
Oral Reading Accuracy				%
Reading Rate				wpm
Comprehension # Correct				/3
Fluency	1	2	3	4

Name _____ Date _____

Bald Eagles

1   The bald eagle has been our nation's symbol since 1782. It appears on the national seal, which is used on official documents, money, and public buildings. The bald eagle is considered a symbol of strength.

2   The Continental Congress decided the new nation needed a special seal after the Declaration of Independence was signed in 1776. Benjamin Franklin, Thomas Jefferson, and John Adams were given the job of creating the design. However, Congress did not approve any of their ideas. Charles Thomson, the secretary of Congress, finally created the design that Congress adopted in 1782.

3   Even though the bald eagle is an American icon, its numbers dwindled during the early 1900s. People hunted the bird and destroyed its nesting habitat to build new developments. Our national symbol became endangered. In 1940, Congress passed the Bald Eagle Protection Act, which made it illegal to hunt, own, or sell the bird.

4   However, the bald eagle faced more problems in the 1960s, including pesticides used by farmers. In 1972, new regulations were put into place, and the bald eagle population began growing again. Today, the bald eagle is no longer a threatened species.

Name _____ Date _____

Bald Eagles

Words per Line

1   The bald eagle has been our nation's symbol since   ___9
1782. It appears on the national seal, which is used on   ___20
official documents, money, and public buildings. The bald   ___28
eagle is considered a symbol of strength.   ___35

2   The Continental Congress decided the new nation   ___42
needed a special seal after the Declaration of   ___50
Independence was signed in 1776. Benjamin Franklin,   ___57
Thomas Jefferson, and John Adams were given the   ___65
job of creating the design. However, Congress did   ___73
not approve any of their ideas. Charles Thomson, the   ___82
secretary of Congress, finally created the design that   ___90
Congress adopted in 1782.   ___94

3   Even though the bald eagle is an American icon, its   ___104
numbers dwindled during the early 1900s. People hunted   ___112
the bird and destroyed its nesting habitat to build new   ___122
developments. Our national symbol became endangered.   ___128
In 1940, Congress passed the Bald Eagle Protection Act,   ___137
which made it illegal to hunt, own, or sell the bird.   ___148

4   However, the bald eagle faced more problems in the   ___157
1960s, including pesticides used by farmers. In 1972,   ___165
new regulations were put into place, and the bald eagle   ___175
population began growing again. Today, the bald eagle   ___183
is no longer a threatened species.   ___189

Comprehension Questions

1.   **What is the main idea of this passage?**
     (The bald eagle is our national symbol.)

2.   **What activities made the bald eagle endangered?**
     (hunting eagles, destroying the eagles' habitat, using pesticides)

3.   **What helped the bald eagle recover from being endangered?**
     (Congress passed laws to protect bald eagles.)

Passage	Words: 189			
Oral Reading Accuracy				%
Reading Rate				wpm
Comprehension # Correct				/3
Fluency	1	2	3	4

Name _____ Date _____

Sleep Tips

1   When you get up in the morning, are you still tired? When you listen to the announcements at school, do you nod off? When it's time for soccer practice, do you wish you could take a nap instead? Then these tips are for you.

2   According to recent medical reports, kids need at least ten hours of sleep every night. To make sure you get enough sleep, go to bed on time. Choose a consistent bedtime that works for your family and is not too early or too late.

3   To make sure you're tired when you go to bed, get plenty of exercise—but not too close to bedtime or your body will be "revved up."

4   To prepare your mind for sleep, create a bedtime ritual in which you do the same things in the same order every night.

5   To end your day on a pleasant note, read a good book just before you turn out the light.

Name _____ Date _____

Sleep Tips

Words per Line

1   When you get up in the morning, are you still tired? ___11
When you listen to the announcements at school, do ___20
you nod off? When it's time for soccer practice, do you ___31
wish you could take a nap instead? Then these tips are ___42
for you. ___44

2   According to recent medical reports, kids need at ___52
least ten hours of sleep every night. To make sure ___62
you get enough sleep, go to bed on time. Choose a ___73
consistent bedtime that works for your family and is not ___83
too early or too late. ___88

3   To make sure you're tired when you go to bed, get ___99
plenty of exercise—but not too close to bedtime or your ___110
body will be "revved up." ___115

4   To prepare your mind for sleep, create a bedtime ___124
ritual in which you do the same things in the same ___135
order every night. ___138

5   To end your day on a pleasant note, read a good ___149
book just before you turn out the light. ___157

Comprehension Questions

1.   **What is the main purpose of this passage?**
(to give advice on how to get enough sleep)

2.   **What can cause you to have trouble falling asleep?**
(exercising right before bed)

3.   **What is a "bedtime ritual"?**
(doing the same things every night before bed)

Passage	Words: 157			
Oral Reading Accuracy				%
Reading Rate				wpm
Comprehension # Correct				/3
Fluency	1	2	3	4

Name _____ Date _____

The Chernobyl Disaster

1   At 11 p.m. on April 25, 1986, nuclear power plant workers in Ukraine began running a test on a reactor, but the test did not go as planned. About two hours later, two explosions rocked the Chernobyl-4 reactor. Workers did not realize how horrible the situation was or how much their world was about to change.

2   During the testing, the splitting atoms overheated. The whole process went too fast. Water in the reactor produced too much steam, and pressure built up until it blew the lid off the reactor. The shield that kept the radioactive materials in the reactor flew off. Burning material burst into the air, forming a cloud and starting several fires.

3   No one realized how much radioactive material they were breathing in or how much was getting on their skin. Brave people fought the flames and saved the rest of the power plant from catching fire. But many of the firefighters and workers died or later had serious illnesses.

4   After the explosion, about 135,000 people had to leave their homes forever because the land and water were toxic.

Grades K–6 • Benchmark Advance • **Fluency** Quick Checks • © Benchmark Education Company, LLC

Name _____ Date _____

The Chernobyl Disaster

Words per Line

1   At 11 p.m. on April 25, 1986, nuclear power plant ____11
workers in Ukraine began running a test on a reactor, ____21
but the test did not go as planned. About two hours ____32
later, two explosions rocked the Chernobyl-4 reactor. ____39
Workers did not realize how horrible the situation was ____48
or how much their world was about to change. ____57

2   During the testing, the splitting atoms overheated. ____64
The whole process went too fast. Water in the reactor ____74
produced too much steam, and pressure built up until ____83
it blew the lid off the reactor. The shield that kept the ____95
radioactive materials in the reactor flew off. Burning ____103
material burst into the air, forming a cloud and ____112
starting several fires. ____115

3   No one realized how much radioactive material they ____123
were breathing in or how much was getting on their ____133
skin. Brave people fought the flames and saved the ____142
rest of the power plant from catching fire. But many ____152
of the firefighters and workers died or later had ____161
serious illnesses. ____163

4   After the explosion, about 135,000 people had to ____171
leave their homes forever because the land and water ____180
were toxic. ____182

Comprehension Questions

1. **What caused the explosions at Chernobyl?**
    (Workers ran a test, but it went too fast and got out of control.)

2. **What started fires near the power plant?**
    (burning material from the reactor)

3. **How did the Chernobyl disaster affect people in the area?**
    (Many died or became ill, and thousands of people had to leave their homes forever.)

Passage	Words: 182			
Oral Reading Accuracy				%
Reading Rate				wpm
Comprehension # Correct				/3
Fluency	1	2	3	4

Name _____ Date _____

Frozen in Time

1   Pompeii was a thriving city in ancient Rome, but that changed in 79 CE when Mount Vesuvius erupted. The sky turned black and the city was buried in thick, volcanic ash. About two thousand people perished, and the city was then abandoned for centuries.

2   In 1748, a group of explorers discovered the ancient site, still covered in debris. Archaeologists began uncovering the city very slowly. To their surprise, the city was mainly intact underneath. Buildings still stood, and human skeletons were frozen in place. Dwellings contained household goods, mostly untouched. Paintings, drawings, and architectural details were perfectly preserved, and even food was discovered! Experts say the city was so well preserved because the volcanic ash solidified into a hard shell that protected the contents below.

3   Today, the excavation work continues. Hundreds of skeletons have been uncovered, and marketplaces, arenas, government buildings, roads, and other structures have been studied. We have learned a lot about the ancient Romans' way of life from discoveries at Pompeii.

Name _____ Date _____

Frozen in Time

Words per Line

1   Pompeii was a thriving city in ancient Rome, but   ____9
that changed in 79 CE when Mount Vesuvius erupted.   ____19
The sky turned black and the city was buried in thick,   ____30
volcanic ash. About two thousand people perished, and   ____38
the city was then abandoned for centuries.   ____45

2   In 1748, a group of explorers discovered the ancient   ____54
site, still covered in debris. Archaeologists began   ____61
uncovering the city very slowly. To their surprise, the   ____70
city was mainly intact underneath. Buildings still stood,   ____78
and human skeletons were frozen in place. Dwellings   ____86
contained household goods, mostly untouched. Paintings,   ____92
drawings, and architectural details were perfectly   ____98
preserved, and even food was discovered! Experts say   ____106
the city was so well preserved because the volcanic ash   ____116
solidified into a hard shell that protected the contents   ____125
below.   ____126

3   Today, the excavation work continues. Hundreds of   ____133
skeletons have been uncovered, and marketplaces,   ____139
arenas, government buildings, roads, and other   ____145
structures have been studied. We have learned a lot   ____154
about the ancient Romans' way of life from discoveries   ____163
at Pompeii.   ____165

Comprehension Questions

1. **What happened to the city of Pompeii in 79 CE?**
    (It was covered with volcanic ash as Mount Vesuvius erupted.)

2. **How did much of the city stay untouched for so long?**
    (The volcanic ash hardened into a protective shell.)

3. **Why is the city of Pompeii valuable today?**
    (It helps us learn how people lived in ancient Rome.)

Passage	Words: 165			
Oral Reading Accuracy				%
Reading Rate				wpm
Comprehension # Correct				/3
Fluency	1	2	3	4

Name _____ Date _____

Pesky Flies

1   It was a particularly bad year for flies, which were really annoying when they buzzed in Justin's face. "Let's buy some fly spray to get rid of these pesky flies," suggested Justin.

2   But his parents reminded him that while fly spray might kill the flies, it was also harmful to the environment. So Justin began to think about alternatives.

3   "Hey, frogs eat flies, so we could raise frogs in our house," suggested Justin.

4   "I don't think it would be fair to force frogs to live in tanks in our house," objected Justin's dad, "just to make us more comfortable."

5   Justin thought harder and suddenly blurted out, "Oh, I know something that'll get rid of the flies. It's green like a frog and it 'eats' flies, too."

6   "A green spider or a green vacuum cleaner?" guessed his mom.

7   "No, green Venus flytraps. They love eating pesky flies!" said Justin.

Name _____   Date _____

Pesky Flies

	Words per Line

1   It was a particularly bad year for flies, which were   ___10
really annoying when they buzzed in Justin's face.   ___18
"Let's buy some fly spray to get rid of these pesky   ___29
flies," suggested Justin.   ___32

2   But his parents reminded him that while fly spray   ___41
might kill the flies, it was also harmful to the   ___51
environment. So Justin began to think about alternatives.   ___59

3   "Hey, frogs eat flies, so we could raise frogs in our   ___70
house," suggested Justin.   ___73

4   "I don't think it would be fair to force frogs to live in   ___86
tanks in our house," objected Justin's dad, "just to make   ___96
us more comfortable."   ___99

5   Justin thought harder and suddenly blurted out, "Oh, I   ___108
know something that'll get rid of the flies. It's green like   ___119
a frog and it 'eats' flies, too."   ___126

6   "A green spider or a green vacuum cleaner?" guessed   ___135
his mom.   ___137

7   "No, green Venus flytraps. They love eating pesky   ___145
flies!" said Justin.   ___148

Comprehension Questions

1. **What is the problem Justin faces in this story?**
    (There are too many pesky flies.)

2. **What is wrong with using fly spray to get rid of the flies?**
    (It is harmful to the environment.)

3. **What did Justin suggest at the end of the story to solve the problem?**
    (He suggested getting Venus flytraps, which would eat the flies.)

Passage	Words: 148			
Oral Reading Accuracy				%
Reading Rate				wpm
Comprehension # Correct				/3
Fluency	1	2	3	4

Name _____ Date _____

Pluto

1   For decades after it was discovered in 1930, Pluto
was known as the ninth planet. It is tiny compared with
other planets. It is also the farthest from the sun—a
whopping 3.6 billion miles away. It takes 248 years for
Pluto to make one trip around the sun. And, because
of its distance from the sun, Pluto's temperatures are
downright frigid.

2   However, a discovery in 2003 made scientists question
Pluto's status. An astronomer discovered an object
beyond Pluto that he named Eris, which he thought
was a new planet. This discovery caused astronomers
to rethink their definition of "planet." They determined
that these small objects so far away from the sun
were not true planets but instead should be considered
"dwarf planets."

3   Dwarf planets are round like other planets, and they
orbit the sun. However, they are much smaller. In
addition, dwarf planets have very little gravity, so they
can't attract tiny objects and space dust in their path
as the other eight planets can. Today, any planet that
lies beyond Neptune is considered a dwarf planet.

Name _____ Date _____

Pluto

Words per Line

1 For decades after it was discovered in 1930, Pluto was known as the ninth planet. It is tiny compared with other planets. It is also the farthest from the sun—a whopping 3.6 billion miles away. It takes 248 years for Pluto to make one trip around the sun. And, because of its distance from the sun, Pluto's temperatures are downright frigid.

___9
___20
___31
___41
___51
___60
___62

2 However, a discovery in 2003 made scientists question Pluto's status. An astronomer discovered an object beyond Pluto that he named Eris, which he thought was a new planet. This discovery caused astronomers to rethink their definition of "planet." They determined that these small objects so far away from the sun were not true planets but instead should be considered "dwarf planets."

___70
___77
___86
___94
___102
___112
___121
___123

3 Dwarf planets are round like other planets, and they orbit the sun. However, they are much smaller. In addition, dwarf planets have very little gravity, so they can't attract tiny objects and space dust in their path as the other eight planets can. Today, any planet that lies beyond Neptune is considered a dwarf planet.

___132
___141
___150
___160
___170
___178

Comprehension Questions

1. **What is the main topic of this passage?**
   (Pluto's status as a planet)

2. **What made people think differently about Pluto?**
   (the discovery of Eris)

3. **What are two differences between true planets and dwarf planets?**
   (Dwarf planets are smaller than true planets and have less gravity. Also, they are farther away from the sun.)

Passage	Words: 178			
Oral Reading Accuracy				%
Reading Rate				wpm
Comprehension # Correct				/3
Fluency	1	2	3	4

Name _____ Date _____

A Fortunate Mistake

1   In 1930, the chocolate chip cookie was born—by accident!

2   Ruth Wakefield was a dietitian and food lecturer from Boston. Ruth enjoyed cooking, so she and her husband purchased a roadside inn called "The Toll House Inn." Travelers could stay overnight and enjoy home-cooked meals Ruth prepared for them.

3   One day, Ruth was making chocolate cookies and realized that she had run out of baker's chocolate. All she had on hand was a solid chocolate bar, so she broke it up and put it into her batter. Ruth thought the chocolate would melt into the batter, but the cookies came out of the oven containing solid chocolate chunks. Ruth served them to her guests anyway, and they loved these new "Toll House Crunch Cookies."

4   The cookies became very popular locally. Then more people found out about them when a Boston newspaper published an article. Ruth's cookies became famous. Today, chocolate chip cookies are still the most popular cookie in the country.

Name _____ Date _____

A Fortunate Mistake

Words per Line

1   In 1930, the chocolate chip cookie was born—by
accident!

____9
____10

2   Ruth Wakefield was a dietitian and food lecturer from
Boston. Ruth enjoyed cooking, so she and her husband
purchased a roadside inn called "The Toll House Inn."
Travelers could stay overnight and enjoy home-cooked
meals Ruth prepared for them.

____19
____28
____37
____44
____49

3   One day, Ruth was making chocolate cookies and
realized that she had run out of baker's chocolate. All
she had on hand was a solid chocolate bar, so she
broke it up and put it into her batter. Ruth thought the
chocolate would melt into the batter, but the cookies
came out of the oven containing solid chocolate chunks.
Ruth served them to her guests anyway, and they loved
these new "Toll House Crunch Cookies."

____57
____67
____78
____90
____99
____108
____118
____124

4   The cookies became very popular locally. Then more
people found out about them when a Boston newspaper
published an article. Ruth's cookies became famous.
Today, chocolate chip cookies are still the most popular
cookie in the country.

____132
____141
____148
____157
____161

Comprehension Questions

1.   **What is the main idea of this passage?**
(*Ruth Wakefield invented chocolate chip cookies by accident.*)

2.   **What did Ruth do with her first batch of cookies?**
(*She served them to her guests.*)

3.   **Why did Ruth call her cookies "Toll House Crunch Cookies"?**
(*She named them after her inn.*)

Passage	Words: 161			
Oral Reading Accuracy				%
Reading Rate				wpm
Comprehension # Correct				/3
Fluency	1	2	3	4

Name _____ Date _____

Land Sailing

1   Most weekends, Lara and her family go land sailing on the dry lake bed in a nearby desert.

2   "Remember your helmet and gloves, Lara. You got enormous blisters and rope burns on your hands when you last went land sailing without gloves," said her mom.

3   "I'm going to see if I can improve on my speed record from last weekend by at least a few miles per hour," said Lara's brother, Reggie.

4   "I'm going to practice my favorite trick—lifting one side of my dirtboat off the ground while zooming along on just two wheels," said Lara.

5   "You kids are speedsters and tricksters, just like your mom," said Dad.

6   "You were the national dirtboat champion for two years in a row, Dad. I think we take after you!" said Reggie.

7   "Yes, but your mother taught me everything I know about dirtboats!" said Dad, laughing.

Name _____ Date _____

Land Sailing

Words per Line

1 Most weekends, Lara and her family go land sailing	___9
on the dry lake bed in a nearby desert.	___18
2 "Remember your helmet and gloves, Lara. You got	___26
enormous blisters and rope burns on your hands	___34
when you last went land sailing without gloves," said	___43
her mom.	___45
3 "I'm going to see if I can improve on my speed	___56
record from last weekend by at least a few miles	___66
per hour," said Lara's brother, Reggie.	___72
4 "I'm going to practice my favorite trick—lifting one	___81
side of my dirtboat off the ground while zooming	___90
along on just two wheels," said Lara.	___97
5 "You kids are speedsters and tricksters, just like	___105
your mom," said Dad.	___109
6 "You were the national dirtboat champion for two	___117
years in a row, Dad. I think we take after you!"	___128
said Reggie.	___130
7 "Yes, but your mother taught me everything I	___138
know about dirtboats!" said Dad, laughing.	___144

Comprehension Questions

1. **What do Lara and her family like to do on weekends?**
   (go land sailing, or dirtboating)

2. **Where does the family go on weekends?**
   (a dry lake bed in a nearby desert)

3. **Why does Lara's dad call her and her brother "speedsters and tricksters"?**
   (Lara and her brother like to go fast and do tricks.)

Passage	Words: 143			
Oral Reading Accuracy				%
Reading Rate				wpm
Comprehension # Correct				/3
Fluency	1	2	3	4

Name _____ Date _____

At the Bottom of the World

1   Antarctica is a very large continent in the Southern Hemisphere. Conditions there are harsh. Frigid temperatures and bone-chilling winds dominate much of the year. There are no actual inhabitants, but many researchers now live there part-time.

2   Researchers are drawn to Antarctica to study many aspects of science. Climate change and polar ice caps are important areas of study, as is the sustainability of the unique Antarctic ecosystem.

3   The McMurdo station is the main United States research station in Antarctica. It is a very large facility complete with landing strips, a helicopter pad, dormitories, a firehouse, a water distillation plant, warehouses, stores, and clubs. All of the buildings are linked by sewer, telephone, water, and power lines. About a thousand people conduct research there in the summer, but the number drops to around 250 during the winter months.

4   It is exciting to work at the McMurdo station, but there are also dangers. On the first day of arrival, everyone must take a full-day safety class. This class teaches people how to survive in severe weather conditions, how to walk on sea ice while recognizing possible weak spots, and how to conserve water.

Name _____ Date _____

At the Bottom of the World

Words per Line

1   Antarctica is a very large continent in the Southern   ____9
Hemisphere. Conditions there are harsh. Frigid   ____15
temperatures and bone-chilling winds dominate much   ____21
of the year. There are no actual inhabitants, but many   ____31
researchers now live there part-time.   ____36

2   Researchers are drawn to Antarctica to study many   ____44
aspects of science. Climate change and polar ice caps   ____53
are important areas of study, as is the sustainability of   ____63
the unique Antarctic ecosystem.   ____67

3   The McMurdo station is the main United States   ____75
research station in Antarctica. It is a very large   ____84
facility complete with landing strips, a helicopter pad,   ____92
dormitories, a firehouse, a water distillation plant,   ____99
warehouses, stores, and clubs. All of the buildings are   ____108
linked by sewer, telephone, water, and power lines.   ____116
About a thousand people conduct research there in the   ____125
summer, but the number drops to around 250 during   ____134
the winter months.   ____137

4   It is exciting to work at the McMurdo station, but   ____147
there are also dangers. On the first day of arrival,   ____157
everyone must take a full-day safety class. This class   ____166
teaches people how to survive in severe weather   ____174
conditions, how to walk on sea ice while recognizing   ____183
possible weak spots, and how to conserve water.   ____191

Comprehension Questions

1. **What is this passage mainly about?**
   (the McMurdo research station and scientists in Antarctica)

2. **How is the McMurdo station like a small town?**
   (It has power, sewer, and water lines like in a town, OR it has community services that you'd find in a town—stores, clubs, and so on.)

3. **What are two things taught at the safety course when people arrive in Antarctica?**
   (how to walk on sea ice, how to conserve water, how to survive in severe weather)

Passage	Words: 191			
Oral Reading Accuracy				%
Reading Rate				wpm
Comprehension # Correct				/3
Fluency	1	2	3	4

Name _____ Date _____

Garage Sale

1   "Okay, everybody, we have too much stuff we never use. I'm declaring this week family cleanup week," said Ryan's dad. "I want everyone to scour the house and collect anything you haven't used in the past year. On Saturday we're going to have a gigantic garage sale, and the proceeds will be split evenly among the family."

2   Ryan sorted through the stuff in his room and found many things that he didn't play with or wear anymore. His sister found even more stuff than Ryan did to contribute to the garage sale.

3   Saturday soon came, and people began arriving early in the morning like a swarm of locusts descending on a cornfield.

4   "It looks as if our old junk is everyone else's treasure," said Ryan as people purchased their stuff.

5   "Yes, selling your throwaways has been my pleasure!" said Dad as he gave Ryan his share of the proceeds.

6   "And buying new treasure with the proceeds will be my pleasure!" said Ryan, smiling.

Name _____ Date _____

Garage Sale

Words per Line

1   "Okay, everybody, we have too much stuff we never   ___9
use. I'm declaring this week family cleanup week," said   ___18
Ryan's dad. "I want everyone to scour the house and   ___28
collect anything you haven't used in the past year. On   ___38
Saturday we're going to have a gigantic garage sale,   ___47
and the proceeds will be split evenly among the family."   ___57

2   Ryan sorted through the stuff in his room and found   ___67
many things that he didn't play with or wear anymore.   ___77
His sister found even more stuff than Ryan did to   ___87
contribute to the garage sale.   ___92

3   Saturday soon came, and people began arriving early   ___100
in the morning like a swarm of locusts descending on a   ___111
cornfield.   ___112

4   "It looks as if our old junk is everyone else's   ___122
treasure," said Ryan as people purchased their stuff.   ___130

5   "Yes, selling your throwaways has been my pleasure!"   ___138
said Dad as he gave Ryan his share of the proceeds.   ___149

6   "And buying new treasure with the proceeds will be   ___158
my pleasure!" said Ryan, smiling.   ___163

Comprehension Questions

1.   **What problem did Ryan's family have?**
      (The family had too much stuff in their house.)

2.   **How did the family solve their problem?**
      (They collected everything they did not use anymore and sold it in a garage sale.)

3.   **What did the family do with the money from the garage sale?**
      (They split it.)

Passage	Words: 163			
Oral Reading Accuracy				%
Reading Rate				wpm
Comprehension # Correct				/3
Fluency	1	2	3	4

Name _____ Date _____

Can Animals Use Tools?

1   For many years, scientists thought humans were the only ones to use tools. They believed animals didn't have the problem-solving skills necessary for this type of activity. However, some discoveries have proven them wrong.

2   Evidence came as early as the 1960s when scientist Jane Goodall watched wild chimpanzees using sticks to catch termites. Then in 2008, a diver took photographs of a blackspot tuskfish holding a clam in its mouth and banging it against a rock to crack open the shell. Most experts agreed that this fish was using the rock as a tool.

3   Another animal that has been recorded using tools is the veined octopus. This creature uses a coconut shell to hide under when a predator is near, and it actually carries the shell from place to place. Nevertheless, there were still some skeptics. Marine biologist James Wood pointed out that a creature's house is not a tool, it's a shelter. Otherwise, any animal that has a shell might be considered a tool user.

Grades K–6 • Benchmark Advance • **Fluency** Quick Checks • © Benchmark Education Company, LLC

Name _____ Date _____

Can Animals Use Tools?

Words per Line

1   For many years, scientists thought humans were the ____8
only ones to use tools. They believed animals didn't ____17
have the problem-solving skills necessary for this type ____25
of activity. However, some discoveries have proven ____32
them wrong. ____34

2   Evidence came as early as the 1960s when scientist ____43
Jane Goodall watched wild chimpanzees using sticks to ____51
catch termites. Then in 2008, a diver took photographs ____60
of a blackspot tuskfish holding a clam in its mouth ____70
and banging it against a rock to crack open the shell. ____81
Most experts agreed that this fish was using the rock ____91
as a tool. ____94

3   Another animal that has been recorded using tools is ____103
the veined octopus. This creature uses a coconut shell ____112
to hide under when a predator is near, and it actually ____123
carries the shell from place to place. Nevertheless, ____131
there were still some skeptics. Marine biologist James ____139
Wood pointed out that a creature's house is not a ____149
tool, it's a shelter. Otherwise, any animal that has a ____159
shell might be considered a tool user. ____166

Comprehension Questions

1.   **What was the first example of a tool use by animals?**
     (Chimpanzees used sticks to catch termites.)

2.   **How did the blackspot tuskfish use a tool?**
     (It banged a clam against a rock to crack open the clam.)

3.   **How did the veined octopus use a tool?**
     (It carried a coconut shell and hid inside it when a predator was near.)

Passage	Words: 166			
Oral Reading Accuracy				%
Reading Rate				wpm
Comprehension # Correct				/3
Fluency	1	2	3	4

Name _____ Date _____

The Right to Vote

1   In the 1840s, women across the United States clamored to have their voices heard. Men were legally allowed to vote, but women were not, and that angered many people. The Women's Suffrage Movement began in 1848 when a convention was held in Seneca Falls, New York. Women said they were equal to men and should be granted equal rights.

2   Elizabeth Cady Stanton and Susan B. Anthony were two prominent figures in the movement. They founded the National Woman Suffrage Association. The group's goal was to pass a federal constitutional amendment to allow women the right to vote. A separate suffrage group thought success was more likely through state governments, not through a federal amendment.

3   A turning point in the movement occurred in 1872 when Susan B. Anthony and other supporters protested by casting ballots in the national election. They were promptly arrested, and Anthony was put on trial. Her case got national attention and put new focus on the women's suffrage movement, but women still did not gain the right to vote until 1920.

Name _____ Date _____

The Right to Vote

Words per Line

1   In the 1840s, women across the United States
clamored to have their voices heard. Men were legally
allowed to vote, but women were not, and that angered
many people. The Women's Suffrage Movement began in
1848 when a convention was held in Seneca Falls, New
York. Women said they were equal to men and should
be granted equal rights.

___8
___17
___27
___35
___45
___55
___59

2   Elizabeth Cady Stanton and Susan B. Anthony were
two prominent figures in the movement. They founded
the National Woman Suffrage Association. The group's
goal was to pass a federal constitutional amendment
to allow women the right to vote. A separate suffrage
group thought success was more likely through state
governments, not through a federal amendment.

___67
___75
___82
___90
___100
___108
___114

3   A turning point in the movement occurred in 1872
when Susan B. Anthony and other supporters protested
by casting ballots in the national election. They were
promptly arrested, and Anthony was put on trial. Her
case got national attention and put new focus on the
women's suffrage movement, but women still did not
gain the right to vote until 1920.

___123
___131
___140
___149
___159
___167
___174

✓ Comprehension Questions

1. **What is the main idea of this passage?**
    (Women fought hard and long for the right to vote.)

2. **Why were there two separate groups fighting for women's suffrage?**
    (They disagreed about how to win voting rights, whether it was through federal government or through states.)

3. **What event caused people to pay more attention to the women's suffrage movement?**
    (Susan B. Anthony's trial)

Passage	Words: 174			
Oral Reading Accuracy				%
Reading Rate				wpm
Comprehension # Correct				/3
Fluency	1	2	3	4

Name _____ Date _____

The Industrial Revolution

1   Before the Industrial Revolution, people usually made goods like furniture and clothing in their homes or small shops using simple tools or by hand. But the Industrial Revolution quickly changed people's ways of life. Factories and large, powerful machines were built to manufacture many items at once—a process known as mass production. Some of the biggest advancements came in the iron and textile (cloth) industries, as well as in transportation and communication.

2   The Industrial Revolution began in Great Britain and quickly spread to the United States. One of the first and biggest inventions in Great Britain was called the spinning jenny. It was a machine that allowed a person to produce multiple spools of thread at the same time. This machine helped industrialize weaving so cloth could be made much faster. People reproduced this specialized machine and, within a few decades, there were thousands of spinning jennies in use in Britain. Other important inventions during the Industrial Revolution were the cotton gin, the steam engine, and the telegraph. Electricity was also harnessed during this time.

Name _____ Date _____

The Industrial Revolution

		Words per Line
1	Before the Industrial Revolution, people usually made	___7
	goods like furniture and clothing in their homes or	___16
	small shops using simple tools or by hand. But the	___26
	Industrial Revolution quickly changed people's ways of	___33
	life. Factories and large, powerful machines were built	___41
	to manufacture many items at once—a process known	___50
	as mass production. Some of the biggest advancements	___58
	came in the iron and textile (cloth) industries, as well	___68
	as in transportation and communication.	___73
2	The Industrial Revolution began in Great Britain and	___81
	quickly spread to the United States. One of the first	___91
	and biggest inventions in Great Britain was called the	___100
	spinning jenny. It was a machine that allowed a person	___110
	to produce multiple spools of thread at the same time.	___120
	This machine helped industrialize weaving so cloth could	___128
	be made much faster. People reproduced this specialized	___136
	machine and, within a few decades, there were	___144
	thousands of spinning jennies in use in Britain. Other	___153
	important inventions during the Industrial Revolution	___159
	were the cotton gin, the steam engine, and the telegraph.	___169
	Electricity was also harnessed during this time.	___176

Comprehension Questions

1. **How were furniture and clothing made in the United States before the Industrial Revolution?**
   (They were made by hand or using simple tools.)

2. **What is mass production?**
   (the ability to make many items at once using machines)

3. **What was new and different about the spinning jenny?**
   (It could produce multiple spools of thread at once, which industrialized weaving.)

Passage	Words: 176			
Oral Reading Accuracy				%
Reading Rate				wpm
Comprehension # Correct				/3
Fluency	1	2	3	4